(

Infinite Intelligence

Gautam Sharma

(Dedicated to valued readers)

COPYRIGHT

Table of Contents

INTRODUCTION

Cosmic Consciousness is the core of Nature, the essence of everything and the stable, strong foundation of the Universe. It is the immortal , all-pervasive, evolving expanse of energy which connects all mind and matter ,all that has been or exists or will exist in the future. Human perception has termed Cosmic Consciousness in various ways as The Universal Mind, the Essence of Creation, The Supreme Soul, Spirit, o by some as Divinity. Cosmic Consciousness is defined for our comprehension by whatever terminology and form that human minds can analyze and conjure up . From as early as ancient wisdom till recent modern scientific studies show that Infinite Intelligence sustains everything .The unified field connects all mind and matter. Everything is energy and everything is interconnected. Experts in several fields, modern physicists and philosophers jointly agree that Cosmic Consciousness is the source of all forces of nature and of all particles of nature, it generates and sustains all mind and matter. It is the reason for everything and the pure essence of Being. A meaningful and rewarding rife time, human goal would be to align our higher self with cosmic consciousness- a goal worthwhile to strive for and to experience enlightenment - the highest achievement of human evolution. It is also interesting to look at personal consciousness at the individual level. It resides in our brains which are made up of millions of spherical transmitter cells. These cells continuously transmit electromagnetic fields of energy which flow outwards in multi-dimensional space and permeate throughout the atmosphere to set up far reaching matrix of thoughts, beliefs and emotions- setting up the backdrop of our actions which result in our life experiences. The continuous flow of energy is reinforced in harmonious or discordant ways to create powerful thought patterns. It is within our minute brain cells where individual consciousness resides. The grey matter of the brain is the receptacle of the field of individual consciousness and the minute spheres within continuallygenerate the thought forces which spread into all space in endless waves throughout life. Modern scientists have discovered that our brain cells are packed with units of energy, whose vibratory motions under the influence of universal thought force result in the phenomena of thought, awareness, cognition, comprehension, etc. With this background, it can be logically explained how thought forces are much more focused and meaningful in more evolved humans compared to weaker thought forces in humans at lower development levels.

Consciousness is awareness that everything in our planetary universe, our galaxy and other galaxies exist for a reason and wherever there is awareness there is clearly defined purpose for it. Everything has energy and everything has consciousness because energy and awareness of energy are both natural states of being. Becoming more conscious is getting more actively aware that all things are interlinked, which even include all energies beyond the realms of our perceptions and scientific discovery. Expansion of consciousness is related to exploring levels of self awareness of oneness of all thingsin the universe.

The diverse nature and extent of these concepts :from the thoughts in our minds,with the words which we use and the actions we take connected are linked wiith t our bodies, food, homes,belongings, external objects , animals, geographic locations, and everything else around us (covering all categories of things which exist) all these entities and energies hold consciousness.

Whenever you think of yourself as a person who is small and insignificant compared to the unending vastness and complexity of the planetary universe, stop yourself from negative thinking and instead think really, really big about your own presence by reminding yourself that you have over 100 trillion cells(which amount to10 to the power of 80 number of atoms) that make up your mind and body and remind yourself of the immense complexity and magnificence of nature with which so many atoms within you are configured to make up the amazing, complex mechanism that your body and mind are (cells structured together to constitute tissues and bones and collectively they build-up organs that make your bodily systems and all organs which function harmoniously as the meticulous, utilitarian body and mind combination that can possibly solve and create some of the largest man-made wonders of science, technology, medicine, philosophy, psychology, spirituality, ,health & wellness related products and services. Scientific analysis summarizes that all of us are made up of the same stuff of the stars(carbon, oxygen ,nitrogen and iron being the core elements which make up our bodies and these are the same core elements make up the planets, stars and galaxies also. Despite our being true marvels of nature within,most of us restrict our personal thinking through feeling small and inadequate , with the mistaken belief that we do not have any connection or correlation with the planetary universe .However such a perspective is largely a self-limiting myth and restrictive thinking and has been questioned and corrected by the scientifically proven, opposite viewpoint that the basis of all life is one and hat there is unity in all Universe latticed by the unifying field which is the immortal,endless,all pervasive consciousness in all things that exist starting from the microscopic cells to the vast inter-galactic dimensions).

With the unified field of consciousness is the connection between your inner universe and the cosmos. Some recognized ,well-published modern quantum physicists and molecular biologists have theorized that you are enmeshed within the same energy field(lattice of intelligence)as are planets in the solar system , with our galaxy and even other galaxies beyond). More than that, these experts have hypothesized that embedded within your cells is the same intelligence that operates the all encompassing unified field,Once you come to grips with these facts, you will realize that you can impact the field of consciousness from your micro levels(that you are empowered enough to effectively use your100 trillion cells to impact your world that you live in and can influence many others whose lives you touch). We are all gifts of the Universe but as astounding as it may seem, the way we live our lives can be our gift to The Universe. So here is the basis of the profound “Universe Within All” theory : our lives can create an impact in the world. This book will set you thinking and hopefully make you realize that you have abundance ofunique characteristics, talents, abilities, inclinations and experiences- enough to improve your life and make a special difference in others' lives. Your life's calling should ideally be to activate your greatness to make a beneficial difference in the world and for that extra effort you may get inspiration from within as to where and how you can make perceptible differences and then follow through with focus and persistence. First and foremost, prepare yourself by raising your consciousness to your higher self which is the connection to the Infinite Intelligence)The practice of regular meditation and introspection will help you search for inspirations from within to analyzeyour assets, talents, abilities and realize some causes for the good of all for all .The next step is to follow the old axiom”do what you love and love what you do”. So start with mobilizing all your own resources and confidence on things you are good at and start working to accomplish your goals for a good cause. Follow up with activities that you love doing and have wanted to do, but haven't got down to as yet. With consistent effort you will realize that repeating your good deeds will start taking effect and helping the cause that you had set out to do. This book will set you thinking about the fact that we were all born to make an impact in this world. Was it that just because there was a possible Big Bang, did the cosmos just fall into place like a colossal jig saw puzzle and the process of life start from that event on wards? (almost like the Big Bang being the starter log for simple elements being transformed into complex elements and creation of life on our planet and inour galaxy. Or as some modern scientists are conceptualizing that it was the microcosm that built up the cosmos instead of the Big Bang being the cause for all existing matter and life that took shape?(more along the lines of plants breathing out oxygen that sustained insect, animal, human life and invigorated other chemical and biological interactions to build microcosm upwards to the Cosmos? The theory of the universe creating all of us has also been questioned by the concept that theSource of everything was always therThe infinite , immortal consciousness , being everlasting ,

there has been a continuous presence of life forms. Consciousness being an immortal entity has always existed and has manifested and regenerated our lives and all and all that exists in physical , chemical and biological forms.
Within us is a whole universe of possibilities. ThUnifiedField is the vastness of the common basic energy of the cosmos , an unending space of all traits of unity, balance, harmony and evolution. It remains as the matrix or fabric of space time and as the essence of Spirit As discovered by Plato about 2.500 years back and proven as the new version of recent scientific reality consciousness and matter-are both essentially enmeshed and interconnected throughout the magnificent universe and within us thus maintaining continuity. It has been observed and empirically recorded that infinite possibilities exist and freely circulate within the unified field. At the level of atoms and cells , we are constantly evolving , oscillating and growing and the ideal state of being is to evolve and grow along beneficial, positive channels. The infinite intelligence and understanding pervades everything. To connect with such infinite resources, wecan reach within(through well-proven, widely-adopted methods of meditation and introspection) instead of wishing upon shooting stars to make wishes come true that dreams come true.

Following the above logic and facts given, it can be concluded thatthe basic underlying force of the universe is the intelligent energy field of universal unity, harmony, balance, love, life, growth and evolution ,, which encompasses both weak and strong electromagnetic fields, on the quantum andthe cosmic levels, and all other forces of nature, including time and space, are primarily dimensions of reality of harmony are also conditions of state. The principal property of this field of balance is its tendency to unite, complete and fulfill all living beings within a constantly evolving plan. This field is the absolute constant of the universe in that within it, time and space do not exist. Thus, we are instantly joined with the past, present and future of a universe which is in the process of uniting, completing and fulfilling itself.

The intelligence of the participants is the key component for experiencing the unified field- the more perceptive the individuals, the greater the consciousness benefits(the state of absolute involvement with the higher self, the closer to joyful Spirit consciousness)defines this conscious context.within ourselves, one's full range of activities lifetime. The Unified Filed in spiritual terms is the state of Spirit consciousness. All of us have three levels of consciousness: starting from the lowest which is the ego(its about me, myself, my needs and being narrow minded). Above that is the level of the spirit(the permanent state of existence which goes beyond the boundaries of mere physical existence and seeks self-actualization goals as " what is the true purpose of human existence? How can my life be beneficial to others?). Above and improved over these two is the higher self(the zone of enlightenment which aims to connect with Spirit, seeks the meaning and purpose of the Supreme Creator. The level which limits and denies our connection with the unified field is our lowermost state, the ego consciousness. All levels were created for a purpose and help our existence and interaction with others. The me, myself and for one's own individual level(defined as the ego) is the primitive state for the essential purpose of survival, procreation and continuity because our presence in the world has to be protected, our senses yearn to be pleased and and all species see the sense of procreation through multiplying in numbers, we create the next generation to outlive us- all these being necessary and purposeful cornerstones of the ego state of consciousness.

separated from our original state of spirit consciousness and therefore countrified is so basic and essential to nature hat, early in childhood, patterns are built into parts of the forgetting of our connection to outfield and the love and joy and a state of spirit consciousness embedded deep in our being.

One can define ego as an outer shell which over meant to be discarded The Unified Field can be visualized as a grid of great luminescence joining all living beings within its electromagnetic energy field of love. Philosophers and scientists, over the ages have described it as the primary and essential vastness or ocean of : the foundation of all continuing life,love, joy and beauty that lives within us all.

Within us therefore is a whole universe of possibilities. The Unified Field is the vastness of the common basic energy of the cosmos , an unending space of all traits, of unity, joy, harmony, peace and benevolence the unified field is the matrix or fabric of space time It is the essence of the entire spirit. There is no differentiation between consciousness and matter. As discovered by Pluto 2.500 years back and proven as the new version of reality recently consciousness and matter-they are both essentially intertwined and connected and has the tendency to unify all existing matter and magnificent chemical and biological universe within each of us and connect us with the entire planetary universe. Infinite possibilities exist and freely circulate within the unified field. At the level of atoms and cells , we are constantly evolving , spinning and growing and the ideal state of being is to evolve and grow along positive channels. The infinite intelligence and understanding pervades everything. To connect with such infinite resources, we have to reach within instead of looking our for shooting stars at night to make wishes and hope that such wishes come true.

The basic underlying force of the universe is a spiritual energy field of universal love, within which gravitational and electromagnetic fields, the strong and weak forces in the atom, and all other forces of nature, including time and space, are merely conditions of state. Within this spiritual realm of love, such are also conditions of state. The principal property of this field of love is its tendency to unite, complete and fulfill all living beings within a constantly evolving loving plan. This field of love is the absolute constant of the universe in that within it, time and space do not exist. Thus, we are instantly joined with the past, present and future of a universe which is in the process of uniting, completing and fulfilling itself.

The consciousness of participants the determining factor in being able to perceive the

Unified Field, and the depth of one's sensory experience is what determines this consciousness. In that regard, our most profound sensory experience is the total surrender to what is deepest within ourselves, that is, the surrender to love and a joyful state of spirit consciousness - which is the awareness of an evolving loving plan and the taking of responsibility for one's function within that plan. The Unified Field is therefore a state of spirit consciousness. That state which limits or denies our perception of the Unified Field is ego consciousness.

It would appear that the pain of not feeling loved for oneself and being seemingly separated from our original state of spirit consciousness and the Unified Field is of such deep spiritual proportions that, early in childhood, processes are triggered in the left brain which results in a cognition and memory imbalance and dominance as well as the denial, mistrust and forgetting of our connection to the Unified Field and the love and joy and a state of spirit consciousness deepest within us. that the ego and ego consciousness is born - for survival and protection purposes only. A definition of death or the idea of death, is an illusion measured by the limits of our consciousness.

Think of the ego as a protective shell that over time is supposed to be discarded. The Unified Field can be perceived as a lattice of great luminescence connecting all living entities. within its energy field of love. Saints, scholars, scientists all agree in defining this all-encompassing field or lattice "The continuity of all encompassing joy,love,goodness and compassion that exists within mankind.

Within us is a whole universe of possibilities. The Unified Field is the vastness of the common basic energy of the cosmos , an unending space of all traits, of unity, joy, and magnificence the unified field is the matrix or fabric of space time It is the essence of permanent Spirit. There is so much similarity between consciousness and intelligence that . As discovered by Plato 2.500 years back and proven by modern research recently that consciousness and intelligence are both essentially intertwined and connected. With similar dimensions of space and time and have the tendency to unify the remarkable chemical and biological infrastructure within each of us and connect us with the entire planetary universe. It is logically accurate to conclude that Infinite possibilities exist and freely circulate within the unified field. At the level of atoms and cells , we are constantly evolving, oscillating and growing and the ideal state of being is to evolve and grow along positive channels in harmony with nature. The infinite intelligence and understanding pervades everything and is omnipresent. To connect with such immortal and infinite resources you have to reach within and ask with clear intentions what you want instead of looking outwards at the night sky to wish upon upon a shooting star .

The basic underlying force of the universe is a spiritual energy field of universal love, within which gravitational and electromagnetic fields, the strong and weak forces in the atom, and all other forces of nature, including time and space, are merely conditions of state. Within this spiritual realm of love, and The principal property of this field of love is its tendency to unite, complete and fulfill all living beings within a constantly evolving loving plan. This field of love is the absolute constant of the universe in that within it, time and space do not exist. Thus, we are instantly joined with the past, present and future of a universe which is in the process of uniting, completing and fulfilling itself.

The consciousness of the participant is the determining factor in being able to perceive the Unified Field, and the depth of one's sensory experience is what determines this consciousness. In that regard, our most profound sensory experience is the total surrender to what is deepest within ourselves, that is, the surrender to love and a joyful state of spirit consciousness - which is the awareness of an evolving loving plan and the taking of responsibility for one's function within that plan. The Unified Field is therefore a state of spirit consciousness. That state which limits or denies our perception of the Unified Field is ego consciousness.

It would appear that the pain of not feeling loved for oneself and being seemingly separated from our original state of spirit consciousness and the Unified Field is of such deep spiritual proportions that, early in childhood, processes are triggered in the left brain which results in a memory and cognition imbalance and dominance as well as the disconnect and detachment of our connection to the Unified Field and the love and joy and a state of spirit consciousness deepest within nuthatch the ego and ego consciousness is born - for survival and protection purposes only. is an illusion measured by the limits of our consciousness.

The ego, being the lowest state of human consciousness is the self-centric state ,mostly about me, myself and my needs and can be compared to a transient packaging that is meant to be taken off and discarded over time. In the sequence of progression , we can experience the soul level which is self-actualization about purpose of life, of making our lives have an impact on the world and even regenerating onto a life beyond the current one, A select few get to evolve upwards to our higher selves- those who get to be termed as the enlightened soulful spiritual masters. The next stage above is the soul, which is Ego being the lowest state of consciousness The unified field can be visualized as a grid of great luminosity joining all living beings within its energy field of love. benevolence, growth and unity. Experts, scientists, philosophers and the clergy describe this as the Universal Oneness. It would seem appropriate in describing this all-encompassing field or grid as the fabric of immortal,sustaining love, joy and compassion that lives within us all.

Within us is a whole universe of possibilities and the abundance and wide-ranging possibilities arise out of the boundless ocean of pure, infinite intelligence. Researchers have empirical evidence to conclude that the unifying field is the vastness of the common essential energy of the cosmos , an unending space of all characteristics of life, regeneration, sustenance and growth " simply stated it is the matrix and grid of space and time in an infinite dimensional space. It is the essence of the entire Spirit. There is no differentiation between consciousness and matter. As discovered by Pluto 2.500 years back and proven as the new version of reality recently consciousness and matter-they are both essentially intertwined and connected. which does not have dimensions of space and time but has the tendency to unify magnificent chemical and biological universe within each of us and connect us with the entire planetary universe. Infinite possibilities exist and freely circulate within the unified field. At the level of atoms and cells , we are constantly evolving , reverberating and growing and the ideal state of being is to evolve and grow along positive channels. The infinite intelligence and understanding pervades everything. To connect with such infinite resources, we have to reach within instead of looking our for shooting stars at night to make wishes and hope that such wishes come true. The basic underlying force of the universe is an energy field of universal love, within wherein gravitational and electromagnetic fields,encompass the strong and weak forces in the atom, and all other forces of nature, including time and space, are merely conditions of state. Within this spiritual realm of love, such as precognition and near-death experiences are also conditions of state. The principal property of this field of love is its tendency to unite, complete and fulfill all living beings within a constantly evolving loving plan. This field of love is the absolute constant of the universe in that within it, time and space do not exist. Thus, we are instantly joined with the past, present and future of a universe which is in the process of uniting, completing and fulfilling itself.

The consciousness of the participant is the determining factor in being able to perceive the Unified Field, and the depth of one's sensory experience is what determines this consciousness. In that regard, our most profound sensory experience is the total surrender to what is deepest within ourselves, that is, the surrender to love and a joyful state of spirit consciousness - which is the awareness of an evolving loving plan and the taking of responsibility for one's function within that plan. The Unified Field is therefore a state of spirit consciousness. That state which limits or denies our perception of the Unified Field is ego consciousness.

It would appear that the pain of not feeling loved for oneself and being seemingly separated from our original state of spirit consciousness and the Unified Field is of such deep spiritual proportions that, early in childhood, processes are triggered in the left brain which result in left brain-right brain imbalance and dominance as well as the denial disconnect and distortion of our connection to the Unified Field and the love and joy and a state of spirit consciousness deepest within nuthatch the ego and ego consciousness is born - for survival and protection purposes only. As such, death or the idea of death, is an illusion measured by the constraints of our consciousness.

Ego can be best explained as a transient packaging that is eventually meant to be shed. The Unified Field can be visualized as a grid of great luminosity joining all living beings within its energy field of matter, mind sustenance, growth. appropriate in describing this all-encompassing field or grid: "The basis of all sustaining love, joy and beauty that lives within all of us.

Within us is a whole universe of possibilities. The Unified Field is the vastness of the common basic energy of the cosmos , an unending space of all traits, of unity, joy, positivist and neutrality. the unified field is the matrix or fabric of space time It is the essence of the entire spirit. There is no differentiation between consciousness and matter. As discovered by Plato about 2.500 years back and proven as the new version of reality recently consciousness and matter-they are both essentially intertwined and connected. which does not have dimensions of space and time but has the tendency to unify magnificent chemical and biological universe within each of us and connect us with the entire planetary universe. Infinite possibilities exist and freely circulate within the unified field. At the level of atoms and cells , we are constantly evolving , vibrating and growing and the ideal state of being is to evolve and grow along positive channels. The infinite intelligence and understanding pervades everything. To connect with such infinite resources, we have to reach within instead of looking our for shooting stars at night to make wishes and hope that such wishes come true.

From a spiritual perspective,he basic underlying force of the universe is a spiritual energy field of universal love, within which electromagnetic fields,are synchronized with the strong and weak forces in the atom, and all other forces of nature, including time and space, are merely conditions of state. Within this spiritual realm of love, paranormal events such as clairvoyance, telepathy, precognition and near-death experiences are also conditions of state. The principal property of this field of love is its tendency to unite, complete and fulfill all living beings within a constantly evolving loving plan. This field of love is the absolute constant of the universe in that within it, time and space do not exist. Thus, we are instantly joined with the past, present and future of a universe which is in the process of uniting, completing and fulfilling itself.

The consciousness of the participant is the determining factor in being able to perceive the Unified Field, and the depth of one's sensory experience is what determines this consciousness. In that regard, our most profound sensory experience is the total surrender to what is deepest within ourselves, that is, the surrender to love and a joyful state of spirit consciousness - which is the awareness of peace, joy and love in abundance and assuming full control over one's destiny . The Unified Field is therefore a state of spirit consciousness. That state which engages us or detaches us from the Universal Mind.

It would appear that the pain of not feeling loved for oneself and being seemingly separated from our original state of spirit consciousness and the Unified Field is of such deep spiritual proportions that, early in childhood, processes are triggered in the left brain which result in perception and judgment dysfunction as well as detachment from reality through loss of portions of infinite intelligence . It is from this dark tunnel of pain, lonesomeness, despair and apparent death that the ego and ego consciousness is born - for survival and protection purposes only. As such, death or the idea of death, is an illusion measured by the limits of our consciousness.

Of the lowest level of consciousness,the ego can be compared with a protective outer shell that is eventually meant to be shed. The Unified Field can be visualized as a grid of great luminosity joining all living beings within its energy field of love. describing this all-encompassing field or grid: "The thread of all sustaining love, joy and beauty that lives within us all.

Within us is a whole universe of possibilities. The Unified Field is the vastness of the common basic energy of the cosmos , an unending space of all traits, of unity, coexistence,-existence, balance and harmony. the unified field is the matrix or fabric of space time It is the essence of the entire spirit. There is no differentiation between consciousness and matter. As discovered by Plato approximately2.500 years back and proven as the new version of reality by modern scientists that consciousness and matter are both essentially intertwined and connected in multi dimensional space and time and have the tendency to unify chemical and biological characteristics of the universe within each of us and connect us with the far-flung planetary universe. Infinite possibilities exist and freely circulate within the unified field. At the level of atoms and cells , we are constantly evolving , oscillating and evolving and the ideal state of being is to maintain optimal balance and harmony . The infinite intelligence and understanding pervades everything. To connect with such infinite resources, we have to reach within instead of looking our for shooting stars at night to make wishes and hope that such wishes come true. The basic underlying force of the universe is a spiritual energy field of universal love, within which gravitational and electromagnetic fields, the strong and weak forces in the atom, and all other forces of nature, including time and space, are merely conditions of state. Within and near-death experiences are also conditions of state. The principal property of this field of love is its tendency to unite, complete and fulfill all living beings within a constantly evolving loving plan. This field of joy,love and peace is enduring throughout the universe in that within it, time and space do not exist. Thus, we are instantly joined with the past, present and future of a universe which is in the process of uniting, completing and fulfilling itself.

The consciousness of the participant is the underlying element in being able to determine thunified field, and the depth of one's sensory experience is what determines this consciousness. In that regard, our most profound sensory experience is the total surrender to what is deepest within ourselves, that is, the surrender to love and a joyful state of spirit consciousness - which is the awareness of an evolving loving plan and the taking of responsibility for one's function within that plan. The Unified Field is therefore a state of spirit consciousness. That state which limits or denies our perception of the Unified Field is ego consciousness.

It would appear that prospect not receiving love for oneself and being seemingly far away from our original state of spirit consciousness and the Unified Field is of such authentic spiritual dimension that, early in childhood, processes are triggered in tkey parts of the brain which result in a left brain imbalance and dominance as well as the denial, mistrust and disregard toour connection to the Unified Field and the love and joy and a state of spirit consciousness deepest within us. that the ego and ego consciousness is born - for survival and protection purposes only., is an illusion measured by the limits of our consciousness.

This lowest level of our consciousness, the ego tends to keep us self-centered as a protective outer shell that is eventually meant to be shed. The Unified Field can be visualized as lattice of electromagnetism connecting all living beings within its energy field of love. Experts, scientists and philosophers have been unanimous in explaining this as the universal oneness- the be all and end all of existence. -encompassing field or grid: "The thread of all sustaining love, joy and beauty that lives within us all.

Many therists believe that the Universe is constructed in such a way to admit our existence. The Universe, as it exists, was designed with the goal of generating and sustaining participants.

Participants are necessary to bring the Universe into being. Scientists have studied and recognized that everything, right from the protons, neutrons, with electrons that make up the atoms, molecules and entities growing and larger right up to the planets and stars exist to fulfill our needs.

The entire universe appears to be designed for

us, not just at the minutest scale of the atom, but at the level of the universe itself. We've discovered that te hCosmos has lots of characteristics that make it appear as if everything it contains(from quarks, atoms molecules to stars)was tailor-made just for us. because the cosmos is not "too compressed big" or "too extended," but instead "made exactly for life. Everything else is described is due to "the Grand Consciousness" because experts are convinced it's no co-incidence that the cosmos is so ideally suited for us, and many contradictory principles and hypotheses give rise to multiplicity of theories that opens up all manner of arguments for philosophical texts, and other topics that are considered unscientific or mere figment of imagination.

At the moment, there are mainly two explanations for the existence of all we know and everything living that we do not know about. One is to say, "The Supreme Creator created it all " which may be true but may never be scientifically proved. The other is to give credit to the biocentric principle or Misanthropist , several versions of which strongly support each other.

Many renowned physicists have concluded that if the big bang phenomena(if it really happened)had merely been as slight as one part in a thousand more powerful, the cosmos would have exploded far out into space-too far and too fast to allow planets and stars to be configured(had there been the slightest of error, the universe, galaxy planets and our world would not exist as it does) . without bringing into reality everything that is a reality today. The precision and configuration of the stellar phenomena was meant to be for the human, animal and biological life to be as it has existed ever since. Even more precision-like were the extra-terrestrial forces and all of their side-effects were configured ,with exact detail, for micro and macro sized interactions, the formation of molecules,elements and cells planets, water and alterations in one or more of these were made in any proportion or dimension there would not be anything terrestrial or extra-terrestrial in any form or manner.

(with chemistry, biology and engineering (all finely defined)

CHAPTER ONE

You have a unique set of talents , strengths , experiences, which combined with the opulence and abundance of consciousness provide you with an endless stream of possibilities available to you. In order to discover your full potential. it may be be to your best interest to align yourself with your higher self. Once As long as you are aligned with your higher self, you will be connected to the boundless universal intelligence and you will receive sustained , reliable and accurate resources to complete all activities which you know you are good at and receive confidence to try out experiences you have hoped to achieve but had not tried out........ receives an are building blocks for matter,energy, friendly values of physics are built into the universe like as critical for life. its present value, fusion would no longer occur in stars. Or consider the physicists put this number up on their wall and worry about it. Immediately you would like to know where this number for a coupling comes from...Nobody knows. It's one : a magic number that comes to us with no understanding by man. You might say the "hand of Divinity" wrote that number, and "we don't know how He pushed his pencil."

...we don't know what kind of dance to do on the computer to make this number come out, without putting it in secretly!"

Such reasoning is known as the "balanced" unsociable theory The "greater" version says that the universe must have those properties which allow life to develop within it, because it was obviously `designed' with the goal of generating and sustaining participants But without bio centric principles, the strong mankind's concept has no explanation for detailing why the universe must have ongoing life generating patterns. By extending the logic physics correlated they participants are essential for bringing the universe into its present shape and dimensions,

Consciousness is the infinite space of intelligence across the universe.

.

your own mind. Divinity's Universe, as it is imaged in the Divine Mind, is perfect. We see it as imperfect, because we only receive a finite sense-

consciousness, but careful and thrifty in actual practice. The time will come when their means will largely increase, then, if they are wise, they will live on part of their income, instead of living up to it. This will give them a wide margin for charitable purposes, for the taking up of further opportunities and for extensions.

The secret of supply is, then, to realize that there is unlimited abundance and to live in the consciousness of it, as completely as though no material channels existed, and, at the same time, to work as zealously and be as careful as though there were no such thing as spiritual supply. At the same time we must give the world something that it wants, or otherwise serve in some useful capacity, exercising honesty, probity and justice in

consider it in all its bearings, and then dismiss the subject from his conscious thought, is able to increase his efficiency a hundred per cent., and reduce his mental fatigue almost to vanishing point. Instead of laboriously working out his problems and worrying and scheming over them, he simply dismisses them to his subliminal mind to be dealt with by a master mind which works unceasingly, with great rapidity, extreme accuracy and entirely without effort. It is necessary, however, to give the subliminal every available information, for it possesses no inspiration or super-human wisdom, but works out logically, according to the facts supplied to it.

While it comes natural to a few to use their subliminal mind in the correct way, the majority of people find themselves unable to do so. Such, however, can acquire the art by training. First, it is necessary to learn thought-control, so

.

We can utilize our higher mind through stress-relieving activities, through ongoing exchange of positive values as love, joy and a regular practice of meditation.

.

The cause of all action is thought. A thought, someone has said, is an action in the process of being born. It is true that we possess primitive desires and impulses, but these can be transmuted into noble actions and high achievement simply by directing the thoughts and attention to higher and better things

.

Modern research defines us individually as human disbelieving and insignificant compared to the vastness and complexity of the universe. All of us go about with our seemingly petty, routine work on a comparatively small planet orbiting a sun. With this perspective the universe is not concerned whether tiny bodies like us exist or not. However such a perspective is questionable by the other very rational point of view that the Universe itself exists because of us and for us and we ourselves individually, in spirit, are as vast and complex as the mighty Universe. Scientists have studied and recognized that everything, right from atoms to the stat particles from the atoms to the planets stars exist to fulfill our needs.

The entire universe appears to be designed for us, not just at the microscope scale of the atom, but at the level of the universe itself. We've discovered that the cosmos has a long list of traits that make it appear as if everything it contains—from atoms

thoughts have power to draw to ourselves whatever we consistently think about. Whether we realize it or not,we become what our minds focus on most of the time. Thoughts create habits and over a period of time, our habits bring about all what we have imagined and dreamt about. A universe of possibilities resides within us(being our personal consciousness finding connection with cosmic consciousnes. We can channel infinite intelligence to discover the universe within.

This book provides pointers on how we can put our individual consciousness to vibrate with the frequencies of cosmic consciousness. is apparently infinite, but it goes where-ever our thoughts direct it. By our thinking, therefore, we either create or destroy, to give up lust, impurity, hate, anger, malice and thoughts and emotions of this kind. Very well, if this is so, they must go on and learn, through suffering, the lesson which they refuse to learn willingly. Others may say: "Yes, I want to control my thoughts, but how can I cease to worry when I have so much about which to worry, and how can I cease to hate when I have been so deeply wronged?" This brings us to an even deeper cause of ill-health than that of mind, viz., the attitude of the heart. Wisdom over the ages has identified that our thoughts gather energy over time and draw to us the corresponding things and situations that we keep thinking about. he." By "heart" is meant the spirit or feeling, desiring part of man. It is here where the conflict between the self-will and the Divine Will, between the desires of the flesh and the longings of the Spirit take place. The real root cause of all unhappiness, disharmony and ill-health is spiritual, and not merely mental or physical. The latter are contributory causes, but the former is the fundamental cause. Spiritual disharmony is, in reality, the cause of all ill-health and disease. Until spiritual harmony is restored, man is a kingdom divided against itself, which, as our Lord said, cannot stand. Healing, then, must be of a spiritual character. Until this harmony

If, therefore, a man's poverty and lack, or financial difficulties are due to weakness of character which manifest in his work and dealings with others, in the form of inefficiency, poor service and bad judgment, it follows that he, himself, must change before his circumstances can be permanently altered for the better. The difficulty in dealing with unsuccessful people is in getting them to realize that they, themselves, are the cause of a Until, however, they do realize this, their case is hopeless, and it is impossible to help them, but when they acknowledge that the fault is theirs, they can be shown that there is a remedy for their ills and a way out of their difficulties, by means of self-improvement. Let them then search for hidden weaknesses, and build up those weak places in their character, such as lack of grit, determination, steadfastness, persistence, patience, probity, decision, which are the cause of their troubles, and they will find that their circumstances will gradually change for the better. Everything comes from within—first within, then out, this is the law—therefore the change must always take place within.

circumstances; now let us think, for a moment, about the Mind that is Infinite. The whole universe, which is, of course, infinite in extent, has its origin in the Divine Mind, and is contained within this Infinite Mind, just in the same way that you can hold a mental picture in your own mind. Divinity's Universe, as it is imaged in the Divine Mind, is perfect. We see it as imperfect, because we only receive a finite sense-perception of that which is perfect and infinite, from this forming, in our minds, an image that is necessarily imperfect and finite, which we project outwards, and, not knowing any better, think is real. But the universe, as imaged in the Divine Mind, and as it actually is in reality, is both infinite and perfect: it is also infinitely perfect. There is no poverty or lack in a universe that is infinitely perfect, whole and complete in the Divine Mind. Poverty and lack

We cannot, in a little elementary work of this kind, go more deeply into this extremely fascinating subject. Sufficient if we say here that the only Reality is infinite perfection and wholeness, therefore there cannot be any lack at all (in reality). The obvious lack and poverty that we see around us are the product of the human mind. Those who live in a consciousness of poverty and lack, go through life closely fettered by limitation. They can never escape from poverty, it dogs their footsteps like their shadow. In fact, it is a shadow or reflection, in the outer life, of their state of mind and mental attitude.

over. The truth is, of course, that the source of supply is Spiritual, and therefore

Personal consciousness is being aware of our responsibilies. Whether we all believe in it or not, spirituality is the of human consciousness. The tenets of spirituality are common among all countries, all faiths, all religions: Nature provides for all , what goes around ,comes around, love begets love, hate begets hate , nature has enough abundance to meet everybody's needs, do unto others what you expect others to do to you, treat everybody as equals, protect everything that belongs to everybody, act to provide comfort and help to others and help reduce others' pain and discomfort.

an atmosphere of abundant supply. We have to remember that the change in consciousness must take place first and become well-established, before its effects can be seen to manifest in the outer life.

The entering of this higher consciousness where we know and realize the truth, viz., that the Source of all our supply is Spirit, and that the Divine Source is limitless, is not easy, although it is less difficult to some than to others. It demands constant mental activity and watchfulness: it requires persistence and perseverance in right thinking, yet it is possible to those who are in earnest. By living in the consciousness of Divinity's Supply and exercising a lively faith, the life becomes affected, principally due to both conscious and unconscious change of action.

appears, on the surface, to be very wasteful

and prodigal, but, actually, she never wastes anything, if it can be avoided. Therefore, the action of the disciples was in accord with universal law. What a lesson for us! To be careful and saving is a mark of superiority both in mind and character. The wastefulness of the helpless poor is notorious. Those who are "well to do" are far more careful and conserving than the very poor. There are exceptions, it is true, money has not it in him to command success in life. Inability to deny himself certain things shows a weakness of character and lack of purpose which make success impossible. It is always the start that is difficult: if you cannot overcome the preliminary difficulties you have not the steadfast purpose to hold your own in the battle of life. On the other hand, once the initial difficulties have been overcome, it is not difficult to get your barque into the currents of prosperity. When once you realize that there is unlimited abundance in which you can share: when once you learn to live in the consciousness of this abundance, at the same time living within your present income and doing your present work as well as it is possible for it to be done, you have set out on the path to affluence. One who realizes and really believes that there is abundance and plenty for him, puts into operation a powerful law which will surely bring opportunity to him, sooner or later. Many, however, ruin their hopes by not knowing that for a time they must live a kind of double life. They must be opulent in consciousness, but careful and thrifty in actual practice. The time will come when their means will largely increase, then, if they are wise, they up to it. This will give them a wide margin for charitable purposes, for the taking up of further opportunities and for extensions. nothing, owing to lavish private expenditure, or they have to let other people in to share their schemes who, in addition to taking a large share of the profits may prove a serious handicap and hindrance in other ways.

While in its essence, the Source of Supply is spiritual, it comes to us through material channels, and, in order to have a share in it, it is necessary to earn it. We have to give something in exchange for what we draw from life in the way of supply. We must give in order to receive, and what we give must be something that the world wants or needs.

The secret of supply is, then, to realize that there is unlimited abundance and to live in the consciousness of it, as completely as though no material channels existed, and, at the same time, to work as zealously and be as careful as though there were no such thing as spiritual supply. At the same time we must give the world something that

The subliminal mind is the mind of Nature. It possesses extraordinary powers and intelligence, but no inspiration. It is instinctive: it is animal: it is natural: but there is nothing Divinity-like about it—it is of the earth and the physical plane. It can be described as the inner forces of Nature resident within our body. Having said this we have said nearly all there is to be said about the subliminal, yet this is the mind of which some people have made a veritable Divinity.

The subliminal mind can be utilized to be the problem solver and stress reliever with a bit of training and consistent practice, is a very good friend, reducing all repeated thoughts and actions into habit, which, in time, become settled and part of the very life itself. Thus, by conscious right thinking and conscious right action, a good habit is formed, which becomes, in course of time, practically automatic. This, of course, builds up the character, which, in turn, affects the life. It will be seen then, how important is the right use of this willing and faithful servant. It is no Divinity, it has no inspiration, but it is a very useful servant, as we shall see.

Most of our actions or movements are done or made subliminally. The reason that "practice makes perfect" is that the subliminal mind playing. Many players, some better than others, can play the most difficult classical music without consciously recalling it to mind. As soon as they try to remember the whole "piece" leaves them, but as long as they leave the whole matter to the subliminal (where experiences are recorded and archived) they can keep on playing. I and my subliminal mind are not doing much of the actual writing of this book. We think the thoughts and have something to do with the formation of the sentences, but the subliminal mind writes them down. If I had to think of each word and letter, my task would be hopeless, and I should

The subliminal mind, however, is a very powerful resource and aallyfor it does the bulk of our thinking, and can be taught to do a great deal more. If we had to think everything out laboriously, according to the laws of logic, life would be unbearable. Instead of this our subliminal mind does the bulk or our thinking, and, if we give it a chance, will do it in an extremely accurate manner, strictly according to the laws of logic and without the slightest fatigue. The more that we train the subliminal to do our ordinary thinking for us, the less we suffer from fatigue. Fatigue is unknown to the subliminal mind, therefore we can never tire it or overwork it.

The subliminal mind can be made to do more and more work for us if we will delegate definite work for it to deal with. Instead of laboriously working out his problems and worrying and scheming over them, he simply dismisses them to his subliminal mind to be dealt with by a master mind which works unceasingly, with great rapidity, extreme accuracy and entirely without effort. It is necessary, however, to give the subliminal every available information, for it possesses no inspiration or super-human wisdom, but works out logically, according to the facts supplied to it.

This great, natural, untiring "mind downstairs," as it has been called, is also capable of doing even more useful work still. A writer or speaker, or preacher can collect notes and ideas for his article, book, speech or sermon, and pass them down to his subliminal mind with orders that they be arranged in suitable order, division, sub-division and so on. When he comes either to write or prepare the notes of his speech or sermon, he will find all the work done for him, and all that he has to do is to write it down, entirely without effort or fatigue.

All that he need do is to submit the facts to the "greater mind downstairs," and all the planning will be done for him, entirely without effort, and far more efficiently than he would have done it through laborious conscious thinking.

works it out, and presents it to the conscious mind for judgment.

Yet again, an inventor or one who is constructing something mechanical, can make use of the subliminal mind in precisely the same way. Let him sum up the whole problem,

positions, and who bear immense burdens without strain, worry or care. Responsibility sits lightly upon them, and they are serene and untroubled when in positions, and when confronted by tasks and difficulties, such as would drive an ordinary individual out of his mind. Such men develop their powers of attention and concentration (anyone who is in earnest can do this) to a very high degree. They are at great pains to get to the root of a problem, and obtain all the available data possible, but, after that, it is their subliminal mind that does all the work, and which arrives at a decision. Many of us learn and acquire the skill of utilizing our analytical and problem-solving capabilities. When these capabilities are acquired and in place, we are able to use both our conscious and subliminal mind in a synchronized manner. it comes natural to a few to use their subliminal mind in the correct way, the majority of people find themselves unable to do so. Such, however, can acquire the art by training. First, it is necessary to learn thought-control, so as to be able to take up a problem or dismiss it entirely from the mind at will. When a problem is passed on to the subliminal to be worked out, the subject must be dismissed entirely from the conscious mind. The problem must not be worried over, nor the thoughts allowed to dwell upon it; it must be left entirely to the subliminal. Second, every possible detail and information connected with the problem must be grasped by the conscious mind, and the whole matter, pro and con, visualized before being passed to the subliminal. It will be seen, then, that thought-control of a high order is necessary, also powers of attention and concentration. These can all be developed by anyone who is really in earnest.

A good way of starting the use of the subliminal mind is to hold the problem in the mind just as one is going to sleep. There must not, upon any account, be any attempt made to solve the problem or to worry over it. Having done this, dismiss the whole matter to your subliminal mind, and in most cases you will find in the

This, of course, is only one of the many ways in which the subliminal mind can, and does, serve This great invisible force of Nature is for ever working. Whatever ideal is held in the mind becomes woven into the life through the tireless working of the subliminal mind achievement, and you will focus all the invisible inward forces of Nature upon its . If you will direct your attention into the right channel, backing it up with energetic, conscious action, your subliminal will help you day and night, thus making success and achievement possible.

We have already seen that the subliminal mind, wonderful though it be, is instinctive merely, lacking inspiration and what we call creativity.

All inspiration comes from the Universal Mind, via the super-conscious.

CHAPTER TWO

Many creative professionals attribute their inspirations coming from other planets or from outer space. They attribute their creativity and brightest ideas from some source bigger than them, bigger than from earth(assumption being earth bound inspirations can be accessed by every person perhaps limiting everybody's share from a limited source) The ones who have figured it out is that by elevating their own consciousness to a higher level they get connected to the endless resources of Super consciousness and by realizing this they are able to tap into the endless intelligence that exists.

illusion. The spiritual universe is vast and truly endless when compared with the planetary universe. infinite: partial conception of a fragment of it. Our limited, finite conception of the universe is entirely misleading and erroneous, and so long as we rely on sense evidence and the human mind,

For us to reach an enlightened state of being is the highest and the most noble goal of human evolution. You can help yourself, your family, community, culture and in fact the entire world by being the catalyst for a total community and social improvement movement. Since everything is energy and everything is interconnected, let each one of us initiate connection of our highest level of consciousness with the Infinite Intelligence.

The Universal Mind has been created to be benevolent, beneficial,pure and ever evolving. Humans and all other species (even various forms of non-living matter) are covered by its umbrella of protection and improvement. The latter have to merely be in harmony with the Universal Mind to receive all benefits.

our environment is capable of rewiring and reorganizing behavior patterns. Once activated iwith specific parameters, the mind becomes a forceful goal seeking mechanism. You can even compare it to the modern heat seeking missiles which follow precise targeted coordinates and regardless of wind intensity or unfavorable weather conditions, reach their targets with speed and precision Our subliminal mind absorbs whatever we fix our attention upon, or whatever we idealize and it moves us, other people and events to bring about all that was imagined and targeted. As we learn more and more about personal consciousness, we realize through personal experiences that the subliminal mind has a stronger sense of awareness than the conscious conscious mind. tipof conscious

?

habit, but in raising and directing the attention to something higher and better. By this means a new habit is formed. The attention of the

must be accompanied by corresponding right action. Many people make use of auto-suggestion and expect it to destroy their bad habits and build up better ones, but it never will, or can do so, unaided. followed by constructive action. and games. Older people should interest themselves in hobbies and intellectual pursuits. It is only advanced students who can control their thoughts so that they can govern their life forces by mental It is a case of directing the desires and life forces into different channels, by controlling the thoughts and attention. Here is seen the value of true religion, for it brings fresh ideals into the life and directs the attention to higher and better things. The writer realizes that a change must take place in the heart of the individual before he can desire these better things. When, however, this change has taken place, the battle has only just begun, for each one has to work out his own salvation.

At first, then, most people will find it necessary to do something in order to attract their attention and guide their thoughts to subject. Later on, however, when they become more advanced in the science of right thinking, they will be able to direct their thoughts into any desired direction. This necessitates constant vigilance. Each thought has to be carefully scrutinized before being allowed to pass the threshold of the mind. By reversing recurring negative or unworthy thoughts with noble and positive thoughts, we can bring about a paradigm shift in our consciousness. The cells formerly used for wrong thinking and of wrong action go out of use as new cells are brought into use for the production of right action.

This stage leads to one higher still, when it becomes a settled habit to reverse bad thoughts into good ones and perform right actions instead of bad or weak ones. The power of the subliminal mind, which at one time seemed so evil, produces right action more or less automatically. When once the habit of cleaning the teeth is established there is experienced an uncomfortable feeling until

benefiting by the experience, press on again towards freedom. It is most helpful to realize that not only is the subliminal mind willing to be guided aright, if we will only persevere long enough (until persevering itself becomes a habit), but that we also have behind us all the

Spiritual powers of Divinity. The Infinite One sees to it that the odds are not overwhelmingly against us. Our difficulties are not insuperable, although they may appear to be so. We can always win through if we faint not. mourns with him when he fails. The struggle is a stiff one, for it is only by this that the seeker after Divinity can become strong in character, but the victory can always be won. When the one remember that there is a way of escape somewhere, and that Divinity, who is his freedom and deliverer, will reveal it to him if he faints not.

desire for happiness. The advanced spirit desires happiness just as much as the pleasure-seeking , the difference between them is simply that the former, through knowledge and experience, does not search for happiness, knowing that it can never be found by direct seeking, but finds it through service and love to others and in victory over self; while the latter

This desire for happiness is good, for it leads us through innumerable experiences so that the spirit can realize, by practical experience, the emptiness of all self-seeking, and thus learn wisdom. After running the whole gamut of

In contrast to this, you have only to go out of your

There must be a purpose in life, and this must have for its object the betterment of the lives of others, either few or many. The law of service must be obeyed, otherwise there can be no happiness. This may fill some readers with dismay, for they may be employed in an occupation that apparently does no good to anybody. They may feel that if they were engaged in some noble enterprise for the uplift of humanity, then they could truly serve, but in their present occupation this is impossible. To think thus is very natural, yet the truth is we can all obey the law of service, and can begin now, in our present occupation, no matter what it may be. We have only to do our daily work, not as a task which must be "got through," in order to bring us a living, or because it is expected of us that we should work, but as an offering of love to life and the world, in order to come into harmony with the great law of service. Our ideas of values with regard to occupations are altogether erroneous, from the

weaknesses, the climbing to higher and better things. There is intense happiness in realizing daily that old habits are being overthrown, ever-increasing state of liberty and freedom we do not have to remain as we once were, but can progress upwards, indefinitely, for there is no limit to our upward climb.

But there is a state that is far higher than happiness, and this is JOY. Happiness comes through service and overcoming, but joy comes only to one who realizes his oneness with his Behind this world of shadows is the real, spiritual world of splendor and delight. When the spirit, after its immense journey through matter, time and space, at last finds its way back to its Divine Source, it becomes aware of this intense joy, too great to be described in words. It not only realizes that the reality is joy, and the universe filled, not with groans or sighing, but with the sweet, quiet laughter of freed spirits! it also is filled itself with this ineffable joy.

What has all this got to do with practical,

It is not meant by this that he can blow himself up thereby, but it does mean that he can injure himself, not only in this life, but for ages to come, and, in addition, seriously retard his spiritual evolution.

seem beneficial for a time, and its use, . It is seen, then, that the use of the mind to influence others is distinctly harmful if unselfishly. Hypnotism is harmful, no matter which way it is used, and is also detrimental to the patient. Because of this some of our more thoughtful neurologists have given up its use.

lessons learn as a result of its own mistakes. Far worse is it if others are coerced, not in order to help them, but to defraud them or to make them buy goods they do not require, or sign agreements they would not otherwise put their name to.

.

There is, however, a far more subtle way of mus-using the mental and spiritual forces than by coercion, mind domination and hetero-suggestion. This method is equally destructive, and if persisted in builds up a painful future. With this method other people are not influenced or dominated, but the finer forces of Nature are coerced by the human will. Mental demands are made on the invisible substance from which, we are told, all things are made, and wealth is compelled to appear. experience.

Its devotees "enter the Silence," and there visualize exactly what they think they want, and compel it to appear, in material form, by the strength of their desire or through the exercise of their will.

Some followers of this cult may be able to make an apparent success of it, but I have never yet met any. If they do, however, they will live to regret it, for they are merely practitioners of black magic. Their efforts are of the same nature as sorcery. All such methods build up a heavy debt of future suffering, and seriously hinder the spirit in its evolutionary journey.

Entering the Silence is a good thing: it is really entering the inner silence of the spirit, the inner sanctuary where the Divine Spirit abides in foulness. To sim-use this inward power for selfish and material ends, and for forcing our human will upon life, so as to make it conform to what we think it ought to be is a crime of the first magnitude, which can result only in ultimate failure and disaster.

Limitations can be overcome through a realization of Truth. When we say this it is taken for granted that every effort will be made on the physical plane. It is necessary to bathe, exercise and breathe fresh air in order to be well: it is equally necessary to work hard, and to give the best of which we are capable, in service, in exchange for that which we receive in the way of supply, if we are to be successful. If you keep a gardener, you must pay him. The money that you pay him is part of what you have earned by the sweat of your brain. Therefore you exchange the work of your brain for the labor of his hands, and you are mutually helped and helpful to one another, both giving and receiving, and each one serving

In order to overcome limitations it is necessary to know the Truth and to live in the consciousness of It. of the Wholeness of Divinity and His Divine Idea. If our limitation be restricted means, it is necessary that we live in the consciousness of the inexhaustible and unlimited nature of the Substance from which the Creator brings everything into manifestation. If our limitation is disharmony and unhappiness, then we must become attuned to the Divine harmony in such a way and to such an extent as to cause it to be reflected into the outward life. No matter what

emotions, beliefs and attitude of mind and spirit towards life and Divinity. In other words, the life is lived in an "error" consciousness of disease and sickness. First, the inward life has to be adjusted in such a way as to harmonize with the laws of our own being and the Divine raised to a realization of the perfect Wholeness which is the reality. If this course is persevered with, a consciousness of health and wholeness becomes a permanent mental state, with the result that health becomes manifested in the life. The outward life is always a reflection or external manifestation of what we are within, or our state of consciousness. Therefore everything depends upon which kind of consciousness it is in which we live.

One who lives in the mental atmosphere of Divine Wholeness, health and harmony, unconsciously directs all the inner forces of nature into health channels. On the other hand, one who lives in a mental atmosphere of ill-health, as sick and unhealthy people very often do, unconsciously directs all his subliminal activities in such a way as to produce sickness and disease.

Again, with regard to lack of means, this state also can be overcome, spiritually, only by living in a higher consciousness of abundance and sufficiency. This affects, unconsciously, every action in such a way as to bring about a better

that we shall become beautiful and graceful; but it does mean that these so-called drawbacks will no longer fetter us, and that others will see in us something far better than mere regularity of feature and beauty of form. When the spirit is alive and the life filled with love, the homeliest face becomes attractive. Neither does it mean that we shall not suffer but it does mean that we shall cease intensifying these things and creating further troubles by taking life's discipline in the wrong spirit. It also means that we shall be able to overcome all life's difficulties and trials, become a conqueror in the strife, and, in so doing, build up character. Thus the storms of life, instead of destroying us, can succeed only in making us stronger. Thus our fate depends not on the storms of life, but upon how we meet them. If we give in to them, or, thinking that they are evil and not a necessary d

The result of thinking in this way is surprising. The reversal of thought may appear at first to be simplicity itself, and to lead nowhere in particular, but after a time the vastness of the subject becomes almost appalling. The cultivation and practice of right thinking gradually lead to a knowledge of the Truth. Not an intellectual knowledge of truth, but a realization, by the spirit, of the Truth. This is the knowing of the Truth which sets men free. We can then look through all the ages and know that all is well. The heavy burden which has oppressed us so long, rolls from our shoulders, and we become free.

in his awakened state, is concerned. When, however, man becomes awakened to the great truth that he is a spiritual being: when he learns that the little petty self and finite personality are not his real self at all, but merely a mask to the real man: when he realizes that the Spiritual Ego, a true Divine Spark of, or branch

dangerous and are also unnecessary. spiritual experiences and the awakening of spiritual systems are also dangerous and lead away from our goal. Breathing exercises, whose object is to awaken inward powers, are highly dangerous and are to be condemned in consequence. The cultivation of negative passivity such as inhibiting all thought and making oneself quite passive and open to any influence, is also highly dangerous and should be strictly avoided.

One might proceed after this fashion:—

"My body is not myself, but is merely something that enables me to live this material life and gain experience.

"My mind is not myself, but merely an instrument which I use and which obeys my will.

"My spirit is not myself, but merely a garment of my spirit.

"My will is not myself, but is something of which I, the true Self, make use."

Modern research defines us individually as

human bodies beings mall and insignificant compared to the vastness and complexity of the universe. All of us go about with our seemingly petty, routine work on a comparatively small planet orbiting a sun. With this perspective the universe is not concerned whether we as individual bodies like us exist or not. However such a perspective is questionable by the other very rational point of view that the Universe itself exists because of us and for us and we ourselves individually, in spirit, are as vast and complex as the unending , planetary Universe. Scientists have studied and recognized that everything, right from atoms to the stat particles from the atoms to the planets stars exist to fulfill our need The entire universe appears to be designed for us, not just at the microscope scale of the atom, but at the level of the universe itself. We've discovered that the cosmos has a long list of traits that make it appear as if everything it contains—from atoms to stars—was tailor-made just for us. Many are calling this revelation the "Goldilocks Principle," because the cosmos is not "too this" or "too that," but rather "just right" for life. Others invoke "Intelligent Design" because they believe it's no accident the cosmos is so ideally suited for us, although the latter label is a Pandora's Box that opens up all manner of arguments for the Bible, and other topics that are irrelevant here, or worse.

At the moment, there are only two explanations for this mystery. One is to say, " Divinity did that," which explains nothing even if it is true. The other is to invoke biocentrism or the mankind's principle, several versions of which strongly support each other.

It's clear that if the Big Bang had been just one part in a million more powerful, the cosmos would have blown outward too slow or skewed for the planetary universe to have taken shape. The planetary forces of gravity, electromagnetism, nuclear interactions are so finely synchronized so as to keep the physical, chemical and biological elements in perfect balance for progressive evolution universe's four forces and all of its constants are just perfectly set up for atomic interactions, the existence of atoms and elements, planets, water and life. Minor alterations in the process of formation of the universe would have resulted in drastic changes in life as we experience it now, in fact vast differences in humanity as it exists so harmoniously for us at present.

Mustn't our theories explain why we live in such

a highly unlikely reality? Some say, since we're here the universe has to be the way it is and therefore isn't unlikely at all. Case closed.

Such reasoning is known as the "weak" mankind's Principle. The "strong" version says that the universe MUST have those properties which allow life to develop within it, because it was obviously `designed' with the goal of generating and sustaining participants. But without bio centrism, the strong mankind's principle has no mechanism for explaining why the universe must have life sustaining properties. Going further the physicist who discovered the reality "black holestheorized what is now called the Participatory mankind's theory: participants are required to bring the universe into existence.

CHPTER THREE

Researcher Atkinson stated that any pre-life earth would have existed in an indeterminate state, like a mirage. If the universe was in a non-determined state until forced to resolve by participants, then the patterns have to be structured in such a way as to allow life. The biocentric philosophy builds upon scientists' findings and is the explanation to the anthropy counter arguments which seem validated to the majority of subject related experts.

promises of an easy life—for, if this were possible, it would be the greatest of all disasters—but rather endeavours to show how to become so strong that life looks almost easy by comparison (the life or fate does not change or become easier, but the individual alters and becomes stronger), yet, it does show the reader how to avoid making his life more difficult than it need be. Most people's lives would be less filled with trouble and suffering if they took life in the right spirit and acted in harmony with Universal Law.

It is hoped that this little book may help many to come into harmony with life's law and purpose and thus avoid much needless suffering: to find the Greater Self within, which discovery brings with it a realization of absolute security: to bring into expression and wisely use their inner spiritual and mental forces and thus enter a life of overcoming and almost boundless power.

Spiritually, we have the capability of evolving from the ego state of our existence(the ego state runs our life as me, myself and living for my personal life goals only without consideration for others) to a higher state being a balanced spirit(on a level where the body, mind and spirit can harmonize) which can harmonize with the body and mind. possesses, did he but know it, illimitable Power. [1] This Power is of the Spirit, therefore, it. It is not the power of the ordinary life, or finite will, or human mind. It transcends these, because, being spiritual, it is of a higher order than either physical or even mental. This Power lies dormant, and is hidden within man until he is sufficiently evolved and unfolded to be entrusted with its use.

The powers of the subliminal mind are dealt with in other chapters. The Powers of the Spirit are far greater and finer than those of the subliminal mind.

Through the Divine Spark within him, which is really his real Self, man is connected with the Infinite. Divine Life and Power are his, if he realizes that they are his. So long as he is ignorant of his oneness with the Divine Source of all life, he is incapable of appropriating the

This Power, then, is Divinity's, yet it is also man's, but it is not revealed to him until he is fit to be entrusted with it. It is only when man realizes his oneness with his Divine Source that he becomes filled with Its power. Many teachers and initiates lament the fact that certain secrets are being spread broadcast to-day; secrets that, in the past, were kept closely -evolved people may make destructive use of spiritual power. This, to the writer, appears to be improbable. It is true that strong personalities, who have a great belief in their own power to achieve and succeed, draw unconsciously on hidden powers, and thus are able to raise themselves high above their fellows. The use, however, that they can make of spiritual power for base purposes is limited, and is not to be feared. There are others, of course, who are misusing their powers. These

There are also others who spend the whole of their spare time searching for knowledge of this very subject. They read every occult book they can lay hands on, but they never find that for which they seek. There are spiritual powers and influences that withhold the eyes of the seekers from seeing, until they are ready for the revelation. When man, in his search for Truth, has given up all selfish striving after unworthy things, and has ceased to use his self-will in conflict with the greater Will of the Whole, he is ready for the revelation of his oneness with the Infinite. it is the entrance to a life of almost boundless power.

Our higher self s capable of aligning with Source.Man is not separate from his Divine Source and never has been. He is, in reality, one with the Infinite. The separation which he feels and experiences is mental, and is due to his blindness and unbelief. Man can never be separated from Spirit, for he himself is Spirit. He is an integral part of one complete whole. He lives and moves and has his being in Divinity (Universal, Omnipresent Spirit), and Divinity (Spirit) dwells in him. The majority of people are unaware of this intimate relationship with the Divine, and, because they are unaware, or because they refuse to believe it, they are, in one sense, separated from the inner life of Divinity. Yet this separation is only in their thoughts and beliefs, and not in reality. Man is not separated and never can be, yet so long as he believes that he is separate and alone, he will be as weak and helpless as though he actually were. As soon as man realizes the truth of his relationship to the Infinite, he passes from weakness to power, from death unto life. One moment he is in the desert, afar off, weak, separate, and alone; the next, he realizes that he is nothing less than a son of Divinity, with all a son's privileges and powers. He realizes, in a flash, that he is one with his Divine Source, and that he can never be separated. He awakens also to the fact that all the Power of the Infinite is his to draw upon; that he can never really fail, that he is marching on to victory.

It will thus be seen how great is the power of man's thought. While thought is not the power of the Spirit, it is the power by which man either connects himself up with the Infinite Power, opening himself to the Divine Inflow, or cuts himself off and separates himself from his Spiritual Source. Thus, in a sense, man is what he thinks he is. If he thinks he is separate from Divinity and cut off from His Power, then it is as though this were really the case, and he is just actually existed apart from Divinity. On the other hand, if he thinks and believes that he is one with the Infinite, he finds that it is g

Divinity. If he believes and thinks that he is a mere material being, then he lives the limited life of a material being, and is never able to rise above it. But if, on the contrary, he thinks and believes that he is a spiritual being, then he finds that he possesses all the powers of a spiritual being.

The powers within you are infinite and by having faith in themselves humans can be connected with the Infinite Source .It depends each individual to harmonize body, mind and spirit to reach the state of higher consciousness the body, mind and spirit connects him to the Sacred Flame, thus making him potentially a Divinity in the making.

Become aware of your dominant thoughts with the purpose of guiding them towards positive thinking. Your dominant thoughts embed themselves in your subliminal to create your beliefs and habits which translate into your actions and therefore create your reality. Review your thoughts, from time to time, to keep the happy and inspirational Regardless of the present circumstances, replace negative thoughts gently, lovingly with rousing, joyous, laughing, rejoicing thoughts-thoughts of love, peace, hope, compassion, winning and celebrations.

2.Write down, in order of importance, all your

major strengths and your significant achievements till date. If you need prompting, ask a relative or a close friend to help with inputs for recalling traits and events and make this list complete with everything significant. Every day, preferably early morning or late in the evening,rewrite this list and read it to yourself because repeating these in thought and spoken word will make a deep imprint of your positive aspects on your subliminal.

3.Think positively about yourself. Remind yourself that, regardless of your low, moderate or high status in life you are still a special, worthy and valued person, and that you deserve to feel good and content about yourself. Remind yourself that the Universe loves you and you love the Universe and that you are beautiful and peaceful in body, mind and spirit, just the way you are now. Your presence makes a valuable difference in the world, just because you exist.Instead of doing something greater than others,become a part of something greater than us. By attaching ourselves to an exemplery, beneficial cause, we are loved, loving and lovable. This book underlines deleting all negative thoughts about yourself from your consciousness, thoughts like : 'you are not good enough, not attractive enough or not wealthy enough. Replace negativity such as 'I make many mistakes" , or 'Not many people really like me with positive beliefs-and keep reinforcing:" I am important,lucky and fortunate, "I make a valuable difference in the world. To sum up:you are much more than just flesh and bones,You are a combination of mind,body,spirit,thoughts,emotions, confidence, self-worth high goals, so ,build yourself up-to a higher level than your human form(you being more than just flesh and bones,you are a combination of mind, body,spirit,thoughts,emotions, high goals); importantly you are first a spiritual presence and the physical form second. Think in terms of being a magnificent expression ofDivinity leading a human life.

4.Choose fresh, nutritious food as part of a healthy, balanced diet. Slow down while eating since meal times are special-even if you are eating on your work desk or alone. Switch off the computer/laptop/television, feel important by clearing the table and eat food slowly, with relish and gratitude.

5.Make it a regular habit to get enough sleep (aim for 7to8 hours). Instill joyous thoughts-thoughts of gratitude and thankfulness just before sleeping and right after waking up.

6.Clean and groom yourself regularly and well by taking showers, brushing your teeth and your hair, trimming your nails, keeping well-groomed and smelling fresh, wear clean clothes and use deodorants and fragrances as appropriate. Dressing up with style, finesse and finery will make you feel extra good about yourself. Within your wardrobe budgets and options , wear the nicest, cleanest, fashionable clothes- all this will keep your self-worth elevated.

7When you are done with work and social engagements, put on your walking shoes every day and go for a 10 to 15minutes walk either outdoors or in some indoor facility and work up a sweat doing cardio -workouts several times a week or as much as your doctor will allow.

8.Make it a habit of reducing your stress levels using basic, practical methods. It may be easiest to follow self-taught options , learn relaxation exercises like deep breathing outdoors,or some form of meditation which is easy to practice for you, yet effective. Do all these as often as you can. You may also find relaxation with hobbies as tending to and watering your plants or playing with and grooming your pets or other exciting hobbies that makes you relaxed and peaceful.

9.Bring out items that remind you of your achievements and your happiest, memorable times, of people special to you and display them where you and others can view them often-these are to nurture joyous memories and happy thoughts.(constantly replaying happy thoughts and memories sustains joy and improves the sense of self-worth.

10.Add on to your routine some more things that you enjoy. Find time to indulge in at least one or two pleasurable things every weekend.

11.Take up creative activities: any enjoyable form of singing, dancing, art, literary pursuits will bring out hidden, normally unexpressed talents and help you connect with your intrinsic goodness and help communicate with others lovingly. Take part in your circle of friends, local community groups, with courses, programs accessible to you for all related activities.

12.Take interest in your friends' and community activities to lend a hand and help others using your talents, energy, enthusiasm, your caring nature. Make some time for these late evenings or on weekends, because taking interest in others and helping them out will be appreciated and people will be grateful to you. Send out joyful, helpful vibes and they will come back multiplied. It's important to remember that what goes around, comes around. Giving and receiving is an ongoing circle of positive, beneficial energies- you will receive attention, gratitude and respect from others.

Always be friendly, extra kind and gentle to yourself by appreciating yourself, being happy with all decisions that you have taken. In fact, congratulate yourself for taking the best life's decisions in the light of your aptitude, training and circumstances. Celebrate important achievements and milestones and be proud of your value and worth.

Keep company of people who are important in life and mean a lot for you. In addition, reach out to network to meet more like-minded people and expand your contacts and connections. Social media communities are a possible start to get introductions and accept more friends into your circle .Facebook, twitter , linked in are excellent resources; use them productively.

13.Stay away from negative people who draw you down and with whom you cannot build up healthy relationships. You have started focusing on family, friends and more like minded people, so you can let go ties with people you are not comfortable with.

joyfulness and vitality (level of energy and vibrancy for life).

joyfulness, love and appreciation. who did notWhen sharing a positive experience, it is important to select a helpful listener.

To sum up: sharing our joy increases joy. Telling people about our joyfulness has far greater benefits than just remembering it or writing it down for ourselves. The process of discovering, enhancing and spreading joy starts to benefit ourselves first and when expanded further can benefit other as far out as 3 degrees of our social connections(ie benefitingour friendand that friend's friend and furthermore that friend's friend too and similarly keep compounding 3 degrees of connections for every close, appreciative and supportivefriend , which will add unto thousands of people.In turn, others too can help support more people's joy by encouraging them to share their most positive happenings, and the things they feel grateful for. Supporting a friend or acquaintance's well-being in turn may enhance not only ourselves but other friends and acquaintances as well.

A study suggests that we have multiple times more positive happenings than negative. Why do we not emphasize on the positive events and build upon the past to experience similar ones in the future?What stops from experiencing, extending, and expanding our joy? Relevant research has been done and results may seem surprising because many people mostly hold back talking about their state of abundant lives. They feel others would get jealous because some get good things in life while a large majority get by with mediocrity and thousands-millions, around the world, even live poor lives. We do not want to attract bad luck. Sometimes we don't want to be our own bad omen We may even feel guilty that good things are happening to us in the face of mediocrity and suffering in parts of the world.

Dr Wheeler has shown that making daily lists of the things you feel grateful for—which helps draw our attention to the positive happenings in our lives—improves our psychological and physical health and well-being. For example, gratitude improves our ability to connect with others, boosts our compassionate nature, make us more optimistic and happy, reduces envy and greed and even improves health for people with physical ailments (even a major illness, for some people. It has been shown that by being grateful verbally we find others become loving and lovable, especially our family and friends and that we feel healthier and happier and it helps increase and sustain our well-being. Writing down and verbally expressing gratitude has faster and longer lasting benefits over just feeling grateful or, not feeling it at all. above and beyond simply feeling or writing down gratitude.

The experts found that people who habitually tend to talk to people they are close with about the good things that are happening to them also tend to feel happier and more satisfied with life. They also found that, the more these people shared their joyfulness with someone on a given day, the happier and more satisfied they were on that day. To decide whether sharing joyfulness caused this boost in well-being,a test group was experimented upon and in objective terms it turned out that t Those who shared positive experiences with their companions and friends experienced a greater uplifting well-being than those who did not share their experience with their companions.

To sum up: sharing our joy increases joy. Telling people about our joyfulness has far greater benefits than just remembering it or writing it down for ourselves. This well-being influences that of those around us, up to 3 In turn, we can help support others' joy by encouraging them to share their most positive happenings, and the things they feel grateful for. Supporting a friend or acquaintance's well-being in turn may impact not only ourselves but the well-being of all the people connected

we have three times more positive happenings than negative. What keeps us from fully capitalizing on all the good in our lives, making us experts have identified two main attitude that keep us from experiencing, extending, and expanding our joy: tendency to has shown that we tend to remember and focus more on refers to the fact that while we receive boosts of joyfulness from new positive happenings, over time, we get used to these happenings and they no longer have the same effect.

Their studies show that discussing positive happenings leads to heightened well-being, increased overall life satisfaction and even more energy.

This studies may seem surprising because we are often reluctant to talk about our good fortune. We don't want to overdo " showing off" or we may feel guilty that good things are happening to us in the face of the others who are suffering in different parts of the world. Sharing happy happenings with significant others and close friends spreads cheer all around and makes us feel more satisfied. with life.

Many studies have shown that making daily lists of the things you feel grateful for—which helps draw our attention to the positive happenings in our lives—improves our psychological and physical health and well-being. For example, gratitude improves our ability to connect with others, increases our compassionate feelings and make us upbeat and more positive ; cutting down on envy and greed and even improves health for people with physical ailments (severe disease in one case). on gratitude to show that verbally expressing the gratitude we feel to people close to us helps increase and sustain our well-being above and beyond simply feeling or writing down gratitude. known that joyfulness

The experts found that people who habitually tend to talk to people they are close with about the good things that are happening to them also tend to feel happier and more satisfied with life. They also found that, the more these people shared their joyfulness with someone on a given day, the happier and more satisfied they were on that day. To decide whether sharing joyfulness caused this boost in well-being, the asked to write a positive experience or a neutral experience like a fact they had learned in class and either share it with their companion or not. Those that shared a positive experience with their companion experienced a greater boost in well-being than those who did not share topics of general nature) that enhance swell being.

. Sharing good news helps in a big way, though

only people who are appreciative and at the very least good listeners. Staying away from nasty and negative people is a good idea in this context.

Another relevant tip is to share uplifting, joyous news as early as possible and convenient because over time it would loose its exciting and vibrant impact. networking happier and more satisfied with life. They also found that, the more these people shared their joyfulness with someone on a given day, the happier and more satisfied they were on that day. To determine whether sharing joyfulness caused this boost in well-being, experience or a neutral experienced a greater boost in well-being than those who did not share their experience with their companion or who shared a neutral experience with their companion. These findings suggest that it is the act of sharing joyfulness (and not of just thinking about joyfulness but not sharing it, or of sharing neutral information) that boosts well being.

One reason that the study asked The study group The study group to share their experience with close friends or romantic companions may come from the fact that these people may be more likely to support us. In the study's last experiment, the experts noticed that received constructive, encouraging, enthusiastic and positive messages after a successful experience (high achievement on a test) showed greater signs of joyfulness, love and appreciation. A worthwhile point to keep in mind is that as more and more joy is generated, we have to keep it away from it turning sour, mainly by being appreciative of this noble quality and secondly by not exposing or sharing it with negative people who may dampen the good effects of joyousness. A worthwhile point to keep in mind is that as more and more joy is generated, we have to keep it away from it turning sour, mainly by being appreciative of this noble quality and secondly by not exposing or sharing it with negative people who may dampen the good effects of joyousness. When sharing a positive experience, it is important to select a helpful listener.

them to share their most positive happenings, and the things they feel grateful for. Supporting a friend or acquaintance's well-being in turn may impact not only ourselves but the well-being of all the people connected

The experts found that people who habitually tend to talk to people they are close with about the good things that are happening to them also tend to feel happier and more satisfied with life. They also found that, the more these people shared their joyfulness with someone on a given day, the happier and more satisfied they were on that day. a positive experience with their companion experienced a greater boost in well-being than those who did not share their experience with their companion or who shared a neutral experience with their companion. These findings suggest that it is the act of sharing joyfulness (and not of just thinking about

When sharing a positive experience, it is important to select a helpful listener.

To sum up: by exchanging positive happenings, resulted in more joyfulness. Telling people about our joyous euphoria has far greater benefits than just remembering it or writing it down for ourselves. This study may also help clearly corroborate findings that have shown that our well-being influences others also,that of those around us, connected by three degrees of social networking . For going towards a long-term state of joyfulness, it's helping ourselves as well as others pursue not just for . In turn, we can help support others' joy by encouraging them to share their most positive happenings, and the things they feel grateful for. Supporting a friend or acquaintance's well-being in turn may impact not only ourselves but the well-being of all the people connected to winner. No wonder , joy has been defined as a divine virtue because it expands and benefits ourselves as well as the entire circle of like-minded people as and when we share joy.

The abundance of joy, from an unending, limitless source, is truly amazing!

This studies may seem surprising because we are often reluctant to talk about our good fortune. We don't want to show off. Sometimes we don't want to attract bad luck to ourselves. Or we may feel guilty that good things are happening to us in the face of the suffering that exists in other people's lives. idle gossip and complaining, feeling negative or even gossip somehow feels more proper, practical and erroneously feasible. However, and colleague's studies suggests that describing our happy happenings to close friends and loved ones encourages and uplifts all concerned.

Many studies have shown that making daily lists of the things you feel grateful for—which helps draw our attention to the positive happenings in our lives—improves our psychological and physical health and well-being. For example, gratitude improves our ability to connect with others, boosts our compassionate nature make us optimistic and happier, decreases envy and materialism and even improves health for people with physical ailments (lung diseases disorders, in two patients). new study, however, extends studies on gratitude to show that verbally expressing the gratitude we feel to people close to us helps increase and sustain our well-being above and beyond simply feeling or writing down gratitude. Wisdom over the ages has recorded with conviction that joyousness expands through sharing.

Experts have found that people who often choose to relate with people they are close with about the good things that are happening to them also tend to feel happier and more satisfied with life. They also found that, the more these people shared their joyfulness with someone on a given day, the happier and more satisfied they were on that day Its been determined that sharing joyfulness caused re-resurgence well-being,health and vitality experience with their companion or who shared a neutral experience with their companion. These findings suggest that it is the act of sharing joyfulness (and not of just thinking about joyfulness but not sharing it, or of sharing neutral information) that boosts well-being.

Those who shared their grateful happenings with their companion reported greater satisfaction with life, joyfulness and vitality (level of energy and stamina).

When sharing a positive experience, it is important to select a helpful listener.

CHAPTER FOUR

The basic premise of personal and social psychology is:sharing our joy increases joy. Telling people about our joyfulness has far greater benefits than just remembering it or writing it down for ourselves. This studies may also help partly explain studies by Rick Masters/ Ronald Simmons Being enthused with joy within , by increasing its flow to radiate outwards and around to other people, we can positively enhance the lives of people who are inter-linked up to three degrees of connections away from us, thus reaching a wide circle of extended family, relatives and friends within several social circles and unto communities at large and located nearby or in other cities as well. All those affected can in turn, can help support each others, setting up a reciprocal supporting others' energies resulting in a multitude of people strengthening their healthy, happy living. awareness of healthy, happy living. Supporting a friend or acquaintance's well-being in turn may impact not only ourselves but the well-

Positive happenings occur every day, yet we don't always appreciate , recognize them and be grateful to the Universe. Most of us have so much to be thankful about and proud of, starting with an intact mind and body, food, water, sunlight, shelter and people close to us- with many more tangibles and intangibles, yet a rude remark from a stranger or our missing a preferred parking spot makes us highlight the negative over so many positive blessings. ? A study by Tom Lewis and Pat Hartley suggest that we have multiple times more positive happenings than negative. What keeps us from openly realizing and appreciating on all the good in our lives, which is focusing on being happy instead of being stressed? experts have explained this oddity that keep us from experiencing, extending, and expanding our joy: the bitterness opinions and reconfirmation.; namely The bitterness opinions refers to our mind's innate tendency to give more weight to the negative; Adam Miller had found that we tend to remember and focus more on negative happenings. reconfirmation, discussed in studies on the evil merry go around, refers to the fact that while we receive boosts of joyfulness from new positive happenings, over time, we get used to these happenings and they no longer have the same effect.

How can we counter this tendency to assign

greater weight to the negative happenings in our life? A recent study by Sheila Cole and team-at a renowned university provides a clear explanation. Their study shows that discussing positive happenings leads to heightened well-being, increased overall life satisfaction and even more energy.

This studies may seem surprising because we are often reluctant to talk about our good fortune. We don't want to show off. Sometimes we don't want to attract bad luck to ourselves.. Or we possibly feel guilty that good things are happening to us in the face of the suffering in other people's lives; idle gossip and complaining, feeling negative or even wasting time and resources somehow feels like an appropriate, grounded escape, although erroneously . However,Ms. Cole and team's research suggests that describing our happy happenings to close friends and romantic companions is an important,helpful attitude for health and happiness. content with their lives. Share with those who care is a bold and joyousway of living which binds people together and can ultimately spread out as prescription for an entire community. Experts also found that, the more these people shared their joyfulness with someone on a given day, the happier and more satisfied they were on that day. To decide whether sharing joyfulness caused this boost in well-being, whether with a family member or a friend Those that share positive happenings and joyousness with other compatible people experience immediate, increased satisfaction and well-being, as compared to others who were not outwardly expressive and kept their news to themselves. Well shared positive happenings give ourselves a boost and set up a trustworthy mindset where others can reciprocate their joyfulness as w

Become aware of your dominant thoughts with the purpose of guiding them towards positive thinking. Your dominant thoughts embed themselves in your subliminal to create your beliefs and habits which translate into your actions and therefore create your reality. Review your thoughts, from time to time, to keep the happy and inspirational Regardless of the present circumstances, replace negative thoughts gently, lovingly with rousing, joyous, laughing, rejoicing thoughts-thoughts of love, peace, hope, compassion, winning and celebrations.

2.Write down, in order of importance, all your major strengths and your significant achievements till date. If you need prompting, ask a relative or a close friend to help with inputs for recalling traits and events and make this list complete with everything significant.

Every day, preferably early morning or late in the evening,rewrite this list and read it to yourself because repeating these in thought and spoken word will make a deep imprint of your positive aspects on your subliminal.

3.Think positively about yourself. Remind yourself that, regardless of your low, moderate or high status in life you are still a special, worthy and valued person, and that you deserve to feel good and content about yourself. Remind yourself that the Universe loves you and you love the Universe and that you are beautiful and peaceful in body, mind and spirit, just the way you are now. Your presence makes a valuable difference in the world, just because you exist.Instead of doing something greater than others,become a part of something greater than us. By attaching ourselves to an exemplery, beneficial cause, we are loved, loving and lovable. This book underlines deleting all negative thoughts about yourself from your consciousness, thoughts like : 'you are not good enough, not attractive enough or not wealthy enough. Replace negativity such as 'I make many mistakes" , or 'Not many people really like me with positive beliefs-and keep reinforcing:" I am important,lucky and fortunate, "I make a valuable difference in the world. To sum up:you are much more than just flesh and bones,You are a combination of mind,body,spirit,thoughts,emotions, confidence, self-worth high goals, so ,build yourself up-to a higher level than your human form(you being more than just flesh and bones,you are a combination of mind, body,spirit,thoughts,emotions, high goals); importantly you are first a spiritual presence and the physical form second. Think in terms of being a magnificent expression ofDivinity leading a human life.

4.Choose fresh, nutritious food as part of a healthy, balanced diet. Slow down while eating since meal times are special-even if you are eating on your work desk or alone. Switch off the computer/laptop/television, feel important by clearing the table and eat food slowly, with relish and gratitude.

5.Make it a regular habit to get enough sleep (aim for 7to8 hours). Instill joyous thoughts-thoughts of gratitude and thankfulness just before sleeping and right after waking up.

6.Clean and groom yourself regularly and well by taking showers, brushing your teeth and your hair, trimming your nails, keeping well-groomed and smelling fresh, wear clean clothes and use deodorants and fragrances as appropriate. Dressing up with style, finesse and finery will make you feel extra good about yourself. Within your wardrobe budgets and options , wear the nicest, cleanest, fashionable clothes-all this will keep your self-worth elevated.

7When you are done with work and social engagements, put on your walking shoes every day and go for a 10 to 15minutes walk either outdoors or in some indoor facility and work up a sweat doing cardio -workouts several times a week or as much as your doctor will allow.

8.Make it a habit of reducing your stress levels using basic, practical methods. It may be easiest to follow self-taught options , learn relaxation exercises like deep breathing outdoors,or some form of meditation which is easy to practice for you, yet effective. Do all these as often as you can. You may also find relaxation with hobbies as tending to and watering your plants or playing with and grooming your pets or other exciting hobbies that makes you relaxed and peaceful.

9.Bring out items that remind you of your achievements and your happiest, memorable times, of people special to you and display them where you and others can view them often-these are to nurture joyous memories and happy thoughts.(constantly replaying happy thoughts and memories sustains joy and improves the sense of self-worth.

10.Add on to your routine some more things

that you enjoy. Find time to indulge in at least one or two pleasurable things every weekend.

11.Take up creative activities: any enjoyable form of singing, dancing, art, literary pursuits will bring out hidden, normally unexpressed talents and help you communicate with your intrinsic goodness and help communicate with others lovingly. Take part in your circle of friends, local community groups, with courses, programs accessible to you for all related activities.

12.Take interest in your friends' and community activities to lend a hand and help others using your talents, energy, enthusiasm, your caring nature. Make some time for these late evenings or on weekends, because taking interest in others and helping them out will be appreciated and people will be grateful to you. Send out joyful, helpful vibes and they will come back multiplied. It's important to remember that what goes around, comes around. Giving and receiving is an ongoing circle of positive, beneficial energies- you will receive attention, gratitude and respect from others.

Always be friendly, extra kind and gentle to yourself by appreciating yourself, being happy with all decisions that you have taken. In fact, congratulate yourself for taking the best life's decisions in the light of your aptitude, training and circumstances. Celebrate important achievements and milestones and be proud of your value and worth.

Keep company of people who are important in life and mean a lot for you. In addition, reach out to network to meet more like-minded people and expand your contacts and connections. Social media communities are a possible start to get introductions and accept more friends into your circle .Facebook, twitter , linked in are excellent resources; use them productively.

13.Stay away from negative people who draw you down and with whom you cannot build up healthy relationships. You have started focusing on family, friends and more like minded people, so you can let go ties with people you are not comfortable with.

joyfulness and vitality (level of energy and vibrancyfor life).

joyfulness, love and appreciation. who did notWhen sharing a positive experience, it is important to select a helpful listener.

To sum up: sharing our joy increases joy. Telling people about our joyfulness has far greater benefits than just remembering it or writing it down for ourselves. The process of discovering, enhancing and spreading joy starts to benefit ourselves first and when expanded further can benefit other as far out as 3 degrees of our social connections(ie benefitingour friendand that friend's friend and furthermore that friend's friend too and similarly keep compounding 3 degrees of connections for every close, appreciative and supportivefriend , which will add unto thousands of people.In turn, others too can help support more people's joy by encouraging them to share their most positive happenings, and the things they feel grateful for. Supporting a friend or acquaintance's well-being in turn may enhance not only ourselves but other friends and acquaintances as well.

A study suggests that we have multiple times more positive happenings than negative. Why do we not emphasize on the positive events and build upon the past to experience similar ones in the future?What stops from experiencing, extending, and expanding our joy? Relevant research has been done and results may seem surprising because many people mostly hold back talking about their state of abundant lives. They feel others would get jealous because some get good things in life while a large majority get by with mediocrity and thousands-millions, around the world, even live poor lives. We do not want to attract bad luck. Sometimes we don't want to be our own bad omen We may even feel guilty that good things are happening to us in the face of mediocrity and suffering in parts of the world.

Dr Smith has shown that making daily lists of the things you feel grateful for—which helps draw our attention to the positive happenings in our lives—improves our psychological and physical health and well-being. For example, gratitude improves our ability to connect with others, boosts our compassionate nature, make us more optimistic and happy, reduces envy and greed and even improves health for people with physical ailments (even a major illness, for some people. It has been shown that by being grateful verbally we find others become loving and lovable, especially our family and friends and that we feel healthier and happier and it helps increase and sustain our well-being. Writing down and verbally expressing gratitude has faster and longer lasting benefits over just feeling grateful or, not feeling it at all. above and beyond simply feeling or writing down gratitude.

The experts found that people who habitually tend to talk to people they are close with about the good things that are happening to them also tend to feel happier and more satisfied with life. They also found that, the more these people shared their joyfulness with someone on a given day, the happier and more satisfied they were on that day. To decide whether sharing joyfulness caused this boost in well-being,a test group was experimented upon and in objective terms it turned out that t Those who shared positive experiences with their companions and friends experienced a greater uplifting well-being than those who did not share their experience with their companions.

To sum up: sharing our joy increases joy. Telling people about our joyfulness has far greater benefits than just remembering it or writing it down for ourselves. This well-being influences that of those around us, up to 3 In turn, we can help support others' joy by encouraging them to share their most positive happenings, and the things they feel grateful for. Supporting a friend or acquaintance's well-being in turn may impact not only ourselves but the well-being of all the people connected

we have three times more positive happenings than negative. What keeps us from fully capitalizing on all the good in our lives, making us experts have identified two main attitude that keep us from experiencing, extending, and expanding our joy: tendency to has shown that we tend to remember and focus more on refers to the fact that while we receive boosts of joyfulness from new positive happenings, over time, we get used to these happenings and they no longer have the same effect.

Their studies show that discussing positive happenings leads to heightened well-being, increased overall life satisfaction and even more energy.

This studies may seem surprising because we are often reluctant to talk about our good fortune. We don't want to overdo " showing off" or we may feel guilty that good things are happening to us in the face of the others who are suffering in different parts of the world. Sharing happy happenings with significant others and close friends spreads cheer all around and makes us feel more satisfied. with life.

Many studies have shown that making daily lists of the things you feel grateful for—which helps draw our attention to the positive happenings in our lives—improves our psychological and physical health and well-being. For example, gratitude improves our ability to connect with others, increases our compassionate feelings and make us upbeat and more positive ; cutting down on envy and greed and even improves health for people with physical ailments (severe disease in one case). on gratitude to show that verbally expressing the gratitude we feel to people close to us helps increase and sustain our well-being above and beyond simply feeling or writing down gratitude. known that joyfulness

The experts found that people who habitually tend to talk to people they are close with about the good things that are happening to them also tend to feel happier and more satisfied with life. They also found that, the more these people shared their joyfulness with someone on a given day, the happier and more satisfied they were on that day. To decide whether sharing joyfulness caused this boost in well-being, the asked to write a positive experience or a neutral experience like a fact they had learned in class and either share it with their companion or not. Those that shared a positive experience with their companion experienced a greater boost in well-being than those who did not share topics of general nature) that enhance swell being.

. Sharing good news helps in a big way, though only people who are appreciative and at the very least good listeners. Staying away from nasty and negative people is a good idea in this context.

Another relevant tip is to share uplifting, joyous news as early as possible and convenient because over time it would loose its exciting and vibrant impact. networking happier and more satisfied with life. They also found that, the more these people shared their joyfulness with someone on a given day, the happier and more satisfied they were on that day. To determine whether sharing joyfulness caused this boost in well-being, experience or a neutral experienced a greater boost in well-being than those who did not share their experience with their companion or who shared a neutral experience with their companion. These findings suggest that it is the act of sharing joyfulness (and not of just thinking about joyfulness but not sharing it, or of sharing neutral information) that boosts well being.

One reason that the study asked The study group The study group to share their experience with close friends or romantic companions may come from the fact that these people may be more likely to support us. In the study's last experiment, the experts noticed that received constructive, encouraging, enthusiastic and positive messages after a successful experience (high achievement on a test) showed greater signs of joyfulness, love and appreciation. A worthwhile point to keep in mind is that as more and more joy is generated, we have to keep it away from it turning sour, mainly by being appreciative of this noble quality and secondly by not exposing or sharing it with negative people who may dampen the good effects of joyousness. A worthwhile point to keep in mind is that as more and more joy is generated, we have to keep it away from it turning sour, mainly by being appreciative of this noble quality and secondly by not exposing or sharing it with negative people who may dampen the good effects of joyousness. When sharing a positive experience, it is important to select a helpful listener.

them to share their most positive happenings, and the things they feel grateful for. Supporting a friend or acquaintance's well-being in turn may impact not only ourselves but the well-being of all the people connected

The experts found that people who habitually tend to talk to people they are close with about the good things that are happening to them also tend to feel happier and more satisfied with life. They also found that, the more these people shared their joyfulness with someone on a given day, the happier and more satisfied they were on that day. a positive experience with their companion experienced a greater boost in well-being than those who did not share their experience with their companion or who shared a neutral experience with their companion. These findings suggest that it is the act of sharing joyfulness (and not of just thinking about

When sharing a positive experience, it is important to select a helpful listener.

To sum up: by exchanging positive happenings, resulted in more joyfulness. Telling people about our joyous euphoria has far greater benefits than just remembering it or writing it down for ourselves. This study may also help clearly corroborate findings that have shown that our well-being influences others also,that of those around us, connected by three degrees of social networking . For going towards a long-term state of joyfulness, it's helping ourselves as well as others pursue not just for . In turn, we can help support others' joy by encouraging them to share their most positive happenings, and the things they feel grateful for. Supporting a friend or acquaintance's well-being in turn may impact not only ourselves but the well-being of all the people connected to winner. No wonder , joy has been defined as a divine virtue because it expands and benefits ourselves as well as the entire circle of like-minded people as and when we share joy.

The abundance of joy, from an unending,

limitless source, is truly amazing!

This studies may seem surprising because we are often reluctant to talk about our good fortune. We don't want to show off. Sometimes we don't want to attract bad luck to ourselves. Or we may feel guilty that good things are happening to us in the face of the suffering that exists in other people's lives. idle gossip and complaining, feeling negative or even gossip somehow feels more proper, practical and erroneously feasible. However, and colleague's studies suggests that describing our happy happenings to close friends and loved ones encourages and uplifts all concerned.

Many studies have shown that making daily lists of the things you feel grateful for—which helps draw our attention to the positive happenings in our lives—improves our psychological and physical health and well-being. For example, gratitude improves our ability to connect with others, boosts our compassionate nature make us optimistic and happier, decreases envy and materialism and even improves health for people with physical ailments (lung diseases disorders, in two patients). new study, however, extends studies on gratitude to show that verbally expressing the gratitude we feel to people close to us helps increase and sustain our well-being above and beyond simply feeling or writing down gratitude. Wisdom over the ages has recorded with conviction that joyousness expands through sharing.

Experts have found that people who often choose to relate with people they are close with about the good things that are happening to them also tend to feel happier and more satisfied with life. They also found that, the more these people shared their joyfulness with someone on a given day, the happier and more satisfied they were on that day Its been determined that sharing joyfulness caused re-resurgence well-being,health and vitality experience with their companion or who shared a neutral experience with their companion. These findings suggest that it is the act of sharing joyfulness (and not of just thinking about joyfulness but not sharing it, or of sharing neutral information) that boosts well-being.

Those who shared their grateful happenings with their companion reported greater satisfaction with life, joyfulness and vitality (level of energy and stamina).

When sharing a positive experience, it is important to select a helpful listener.

To sum up: sharing our joy increases joy. Telling

people about our joyfulness has far greater benefits than just remembering it or writing it down for ourselves. This studies may also help partly explain studies by Rick Masters/ Ronald Simmons Being enthused with joy within , by increasing its flow to radiate outwards and around to other people, we can positively enhance the lives of people who are inter-linked up to three degrees of connections away from us, thus reaching a wide circle of extended family, relatives and friends within several social circles and unto communities at large and located nearby or in other cities as well. All those affected can in turn, can help support each others, setting up a reciprocal supporting others' energies resulting in a multitude of people strengthening their healthy, happy living. awareness of healthy, happy living. Supporting a friend or acquaintance's well-being in turn may impact not only ourselves but the well-

Positive happenings occur every day, yet we don't always appreciate , recognize them and be grateful to the Universe. Most of us have so much to be thankful about and proud of, starting with an intact mind and body, food, water, sunlight, shelter and people close to us- with many more tangibles and intangibles, yet a rude remark from a stranger or our missing a preferred parking spot makes us highlight the negative over so many positive blessings. ? A study by Tom Lewis and Pat Hartley suggest that we have multiple times more positive happenings than negative. What keeps us from openly realizing and appreciating on all the good in our lives, which is focusing on being happy instead of being stressed? experts have explained this oddity that keep us from experiencing, extending, and expanding our joy: the bitterness opinions and reconfirmation.; namely The bitterness opinions refers to our mind's innate tendency to give more weight to the negative;

CHAPTER FIVE

British psychologists have found that we tend to remember and focus more on negative happenings. reconfirmation, discussed in studies on the evil merry go around, refers to the fact that while we receive boosts of joyfulness from new positive happenings, over time, we get used to these happenings and they no longer have the same effect.

How can we counter this tendency to assign greater emphasis on the negative happenings in our life? A recent study by Sheila Cole and team-at a N.E. renowned university provides a clear explanation. Their study shows that discussing positive happenings leads to heightened well-being, increased overall life satisfaction and even more energy.

This studies may also seem surprising because we are often reluctant to talk about our good luck and happy circumstances. We don't want to show off. Perhaps we don't want to attract bad luck to ourselves.. Or we possibly feel guilty that good things are happening to us in the face of the suffering in other people's lives; instead, idle gossip and complaining, feeling negative or even wasting time and resources somehow feels like an appropriate, grounded escape from discussing happiness,very erroneously though . However,Ms. Cole and team's research suggests that describing our enjoyable happenings to close friends and romantic companions is an important,helpful attitude for health and happiness, contentment with most lives. Sharing with those who care is a bold and joyous way of living which binds people together and can ultimately spread out as a prescribed attitde for an entire community. Experts also found that, the more the test group shared their joyfulness with someone on a given day, the happier and more satisfied they were on that day. To decide whether sharing joyfulness caused this boost in well-being, whether with a family member or a friend Those that share positive happenings and joyousness with other compatible people experience immediate, increased satisfaction and well-being, as compared to others who were not outwardly expressive and kept their news to themselves. Well shared positive happenings give ourselves a boost and set up a trustworthy mindset where others can reciprocate their joyfulness as well.

Become aware of your dominant thoughts with the purpose of guiding them towards positive thinking. Your dominant thoughts embed themselves in your subliminal to create your beliefs and habits which translate into your actions and therefore create your reality. Review your thoughts, from time to time, to keep the happy and inspirational Regardless of the present circumstances, replace negative thoughts gently, lovingly with rousing, joyous, laughing, rejoicing thoughts-thoughts of love, peace, hope, compassion, winning and celebrations.

2.Write down, in order of importance, all your major strengths and your significant achievements till date. If you need prompting, ask a relative or a close friend to help with inputs for recalling traits and events and make this list complete with everything significant. Every day, preferably early morning or late in the evening,rewrite this list and read it to yourselfbecause repeating these in thought and spoken word will make a deep imprint of your positive aspects on your subliminal.

3.Think positively about yourself. Remind yourself that, regardless of your low, moderate or high status in life you are still a special, worthy and valued person, and that you deserve to feel good and content about yourself. Remind yourself that the Universe loves you and you love the Universe and that you are beautiful and peaceful in body, mind and spirit, just the way you are now. Your presence makes a valuable difference in the world, just because you exist.Instead of doing something greater than others,become a part of something greater than us. By attaching ourselves to an exemplery, beneficial cause, we are loved, loving and lovable. This book underlines deleting all negative thoughts about yourself from your consciousness, thoughts like : 'you are not good enough, not attractive enough or not wealthy enough. Replace negativity such as 'I make many mistakes" , or 'Not many people really like me with positive beliefs-and keep reinforcing:" I am important,lucky and fortunate, "I make a valuable difference in the world. To sum up:you are much more than just flesh and bones,You are a combination of mind,body,spirit,thoughts,emotions, confidence, self-worth high goals, so ,build yourself up-to a higher level than your human form(you being more than just flesh and bones,you are a combination of mind, body,spirit,thoughts,emotions, high goals); importantly you are first a spiritual presence and the physical form second. Think in terms of being a magnificent expression ofDivinity leading a human life.

4.Choose fresh, nutritious food as part of a healthy, balanced diet. Slow down while eating since meal times are special-even if you are eating on your work desk or alone. Switch off the computer/laptop/television, feel important by clearing the table and eat food slowly, with relish and gratitude.

5.Make it a regular habit to get enough sleep (aim for 7to8 hours). Instill joyous thoughts-thoughts of gratitude and thankfulness just before sleeping and right after waking up.

6.Clean and groom yourself regularly and well by taking showers, brushing your teeth and your hair, trimming your nails, keeping well-groomed and smelling fresh, wear clean clothes and use deodorants and fragrances as appropriate. Dressing up with style, finesse and finery will make you feel extra good about yourself. Within your wardrobe budgets and options , wear the nicest, cleanest, fashionable clothes-all this will keep your self-worth elevated.

7When you are done with work and social engagements, put on your walking shoes every day and go for a 10 to 15minutes walk either outdoors or in some indoor facility and work up a sweat doing cardio -workouts several times a week or as much as your doctor will allow.

8.Make it a habit of reducing your stress levels using basic, practical methods. It may be easiest to follow self-taught options , learn relaxation exercises like deep breathing outdoors,or some form of meditation which is easy to practice for you, yet effective. Do all these as often as you can. You may also find relaxation with hobbies as tending to and watering your plants or playing with and grooming your pets or other exciting hobbies that makes you relaxed and peaceful.

9.Bring out items that remind you of your achievements and your happiest, memorable times, of people special to you and display them where you and others can view them often-these are to nurture joyous memories and happy thoughts.(constantly replaying happy thoughts and memories sustains joy and improves the sense of self-worth.

10.Add on to your routine some more things that you enjoy. Find time to indulge in at least one or two pleasurable things every weekend.

11.Take up creative activities: any enjoyable form of singing, dancing, art, literary pursuits will bring out hidden, normally unexpressed talents and help you communicate with your intrinsic goodness and help communicate with others lovingly. Take part in your circle of friends, local community groups, with courses, programs accessible to you for all related activities.

12.Take interest in your friends' and community activities to lend a hand and help others using your talents, energy, enthusiasm, your caring nature. Make some time for these late evenings or on weekends, because taking interest in others and helping them out will be appreciated and people will be grateful to you. Send out joyful, helpful vibes and they will come back multiplied. It's important to remember that what goes around, comes around. Giving and receiving is an ongoing circle of positive, beneficial energies- you will receive attention, gratitude and respect from others.

Always be friendly, extra kind and gentle to yourself by appreciating yourself, being happy with all decisions that you have taken. In fact, congratulate yourself for taking the best life's decisions in the light of your aptitude, training and circumstances. Celebrate important achievements and milestones and be proud of your value and worth.

Keep company of people who are important in life and mean a lot for you. In addition, reach out to network to meet more like-minded people and expand your contacts and connections. Social media communities are a possible start to get introductions and accept more friends into your circle .Facebook, twitter , linked in are excellent resources; use them productively.

13.Stay away from negative people who draw you down and with whom you cannot build up healthy relationships. You have started focusing on family, friends and more like minded people, so you can let go ties with people you are not comfortable with.

joyfulness and vitality (level of energy and vibrancy for life).

joyfulness, love and appreciation. who did notWhen sharing a positive experience, it is important to select a helpful listener.

To sum up: sharing our joy increases joy. Telling people about our joyfulness has far greater benefits than just remembering it or writing it down for ourselves. The process of discovering, enhancing and spreading joy starts to benefit ourselves first and when expanded further can benefit other as far out as 3 degrees of our social connections(ie benefitingour friendand that friend's friend and furthermore that friend's friend too and similarly keep compounding 3 degrees of connections for every close, appreciative and supportivefriend , which will add unto thousands of people.In turn, others too can help support more people's joy by encouraging them to share their most positive happenings, and the things they feel grateful for. Supporting a friend or acquaintance's well-being in turn may enhance not only ourselves but other friends and acquaintances as well.

A study suggests that we have multiple times more positive happenings than negative. Why do we not emphasize on the positive events and build upon the past to experience similar ones in the future?What stops from experiencing, extending, and expanding our joy? Relevant research has been done and results may seem surprising because many people mostly hold back talking about their state of abundant lives. They feel others would get jealous because some get good things in life while a large majority get by with mediocrity and thousands-millions, around the world, even live poor lives. We do not want to attract bad luck. Sometimes we don't want to be our own bad omen We may even feel guilty that good things are happening to us in the face of mediocrity and suffering in parts of the world.

Dr Smith has shown that making daily lists of the things you feel grateful for—which helps draw our attention to the positive happenings in our lives—improves our psychological and physical health and well-being. For example, gratitude improves our ability to connect with others, boosts our compassionate nature, make us more optimistic and happy, reduces envy and greed and even improves health for people with physical ailments (even a major illness, for some people. It has been shown that by being grateful verbally we find others become loving and lovable, especially our family and friends and that we feel healthier and happier and it helps increase and sustain our well-being. Writing down and verbally expressing gratitude has faster and longer lasting benefits over just feeling grateful or, not feeling it at all. above and beyond simply feeling or writing down gratitude.

The experts found that people who habitually tend to talk to people they are close with about the good things that are happening to them also tend to feel happier and more satisfied with life. They also found that, the more these people shared their joyfulness with someone on a given day, the happier and more satisfied they were on that day. To decide whether sharing joyfulness caused this boost in well-being,a test group was experimented upon and in objective terms it turned out that t Those who shared positive experiences with their companions and friends experienced a greater uplifting well-being than those who did not share their experience with their companions.

To sum up: sharing our joy increases joy. Telling people about our joyfulness has far greater benefits than just remembering it or writing it down for ourselves. This well-being influences that of those around us, up to 3 In turn, we can help support others' joy by encouraging them to share their most positive happenings, and the things they feel grateful for. Supporting a friend or acquaintance's well-being in turn may impact not only ourselves but the well-being of all the people connected

we have three times more positive happenings than negative. What keeps us from fully capitalizing on all the good in our lives, making us experts have identified two main attitude that keep us from experiencing, extending, and expanding our joy: tendency to has shown that we tend to remember and focus more on refers to the fact that while we receive boosts of joyfulness from new positive happenings, over time, we get used to these happenings and they no longer have the same effect.

Their studies show that discussing positive happenings leads to heightened well-being, increased overall life satisfaction and even more energy.

This studies may seem surprising because we are often reluctant to talk about our good fortune. We don't want to overdo " showing off" or we may feel guilty that good things are happening to us in the face of the others who are suffering in different parts of the world. Sharing happy happenings with significant others and close friends spreads cheer all around and makes us feel more satisfied. with life.

Many studies have shown that making daily lists of the things you feel grateful for—which helps draw our attention to the positive happenings in our lives—improves our psychological and physical health and well-being. For example, gratitude improves our ability to connect with others, increases our compassionate feelings and make us upbeat and more positive ; cutting down on envy and greed and even improves health for people with physical ailments (severe disease in one case). on gratitude to show that verbally expressing the gratitude we feel to people close to us helps increase and sustain our well-being above and beyond simply feeling or writing down gratitude. known that joyfulness

The experts found that people who habitually tend to talk to people they are close with about the good things that are happening to them also tend to feel happier and more satisfied with life. They also found that, the more these people shared their joyfulness with someone on a given day, the happier and more satisfied they were on that day. To decide whether sharing joyfulness caused this boost in well-being, the asked to write a positive experience or a neutral experience like a fact they had learned in class and either share it with their companion or not. Those that shared a positive experience with their companion experienced a greater boost in well-being than those who did not share topics of general nature) that enhance swell being.

. Sharing good news helps in a big way, though only people who are appreciative and at the very least good listeners. Staying away from nasty and negative people is a good idea in this context.

Another relevant tip is to share uplifting, joyous

news as early as possible and convenient because over time it would loose its exciting and vibrant impact. networking happier and more satisfied with life. They also found that, the more these people shared their joyfulness with someone on a given day, the happier and more satisfied they were on that day. To determine whether sharing joyfulness caused this boost in well-being, experience or a neutral experienced a greater boost in well-being than those who did not share their experience with their companion or who shared a neutral experience with their companion. These findings suggest that it is the act of sharing joyfulness (and not of just thinking about joyfulness but not sharing it, or of sharing neutral information) that boosts well being.

One reason that the study asked The study group The study group to share their experience with close friends or romantic companions may come from the fact that these people may be more likely to support us. In the study's last experiment, the experts noticed that received constructive, encouraging, enthusiastic and positive messages after a successful experience (high achievement on a test) showed greater signs of joyfulness, love and appreciation. A worthwhile point to keep in mind is that as more and more joy is generated, we have to keep it away from it turning sour, mainly by being appreciative of this noble quality and secondly by not exposing or sharing it with negative people who may dampen the good effects of joyousness. A worthwhile point to keep in mind is that as more and more joy is generated, we have to keep it away from it turning sour, mainly by being appreciative of this noble quality and secondly by not exposing or sharing it with negative people who may dampen the good effects of joyousness. When sharing a positive experience, it is important to select a helpful listener.

them to share their most positive happenings, and the things they feel grateful for. Supporting a friend or acquaintance's well-being in turn may impact not only ourselves but the well-being of all the people connected

The experts found that people who habitually tend to talk to people they are close with about the good things that are happening to them also tend to feel happier and more satisfied with life. They also found that, the more these people shared their joyfulness with someone on a given day, the happier and more satisfied they were on that day. a positive experience with their companion experienced a greater boost in well-being than those who did not share their experience with their companion or who shared a neutral experience with their companion. These findings suggest that it is the act of sharing joyfulness (and not of just thinking about

When sharing a positive experience, it is important to select a helpful listener.

To sum up: by exchanging positive happenings, resulted in more joyfulness. Telling people about our joyous euphoria has far greater benefits than just remembering it or writing it down for ourselves. This study may also help clearly corroborate findings that have shown that our well-being influences others also,that of those around us, connected by three degrees of social networking . For going towards a long-term state of joyfulness, it's helping ourselves as well as others pursue not just for . In turn, we can help support others' joy by encouraging them to share their most positive happenings, and the things they feel grateful for. Supporting a friend or acquaintance's well-being in turn may impact not only ourselves but the well-being of all the people connected to winner. No wonder , joy has been defined as a divine virtue because it expands and benefits ourselves as well as the entire circle of like-minded people as and when we share joy.

The abundance of joy, from an unending, limitless source, is truly amazing!

This studies may seem surprising because we are often reluctant to talk about our good fortune. We don't want to show off. Sometimes we don't want to attract bad luck to ourselves. Or we may feel guilty that good things are happening to us in the face of the suffering that exists in other people's lives. idle gossip and complaining, feeling negative or even gossip somehow feels more proper, practical and erroneously feasible. However, and colleague's studies suggests that describing our happy happenings to close friends and loved ones encourages and uplifts all concerned.

CHAPTER SIX

Many studies have shown that making daily lists of the things you feel grateful for—which helps draw our attention to the positive happenings in our lives—improves our psychological and physical health and well-being. For example, gratitude improves our ability to connect with others, boosts our compassionate nature make us optimistic and happier, decreases envy and materialism and even improves health for people with physical ailments (lung diseases disorders, in two patients). new study, however, extends studies on gratitude to show that verbally expressing the gratitude we feel to people close to us helps increase and sustain our well-being above and beyond simply feeling or writing down gratitude. Wisdom over the ages has recorded with conviction that joyousness expands through sharing.

Experts have found that people who often choose to relate with people they are close with about the good things that are happening to them also tend to feel happier and more satisfied with life. They also found that, the more these people shared their joyfulness with someone on a given day, the happier and more satisfied they were on that day Its been determined that sharing joyfulness caused re-resurgence well-being,health and vitality experience with their companion or who shared a neutral experience with their companion. These findings suggest that it is the act of sharing joyfulness (and not of just thinking about joyfulness but not sharing it, or of sharing neutral information) that boosts well-being.

Those who shared their grateful happenings with their companion reported greater satisfaction with life, joyfulness and vitality (level of energy and stamina).

When sharing a positive experience, it is important to select a helpful listener.

To sum up: sharing our joy increases joy. Telling people about our joyfulness has far greater benefits than just remembering it or writing it down for ourselves. This studies may also help partly explain studies by Rick Sandorsky/ Phoebe Simmons Being enthused with joy within , by increasing its flow to radiate outwards and around to other people, we can positively enhance the lives of people who are inter-linked up to three degrees of connections away from us, thus reaching a wide circle of extended family, relatives and friends within several social circles and unto communities at large and located nearby or in other cities as well. All those affected can in turn, can help support each others, setting up a reciprocal supporting others' energies resulting in a multitude of people strengthening their healthy, happy living. awareness of healthy, happy living. Supporting a friend or acquaintance's well-being in turn may impact not only ourselves but the well-

Positive happenings occur every day, yet we don't always appreciate , recognize them and be grateful to the Universe. Most of us have so much to be thankful about and proud of, starting with an intact mind and body, food, water, sunlight, shelter and people close to us- with many more tangibles and intangibles, yet a rude remark from a stranger or our missing a preferred parking spot makes us highlight the negative over so many positive blessings. ? A study by Tom Lewis and Pat McCarthy suggest that we have multiple times more positive happenings than negative. What keeps us from openly realizing and appreciating on all the good in our lives, which is focusing on being happy instead of being stressed? experts have explained this oddity that keep us from experiencing, extending, and expanding our joy: the bitterness opinions and reconfirmation.; namely The bitterness opinions refers to our mind's innate tendency to give more weight to the negative; Adam Miller had found that we tend to remember and focus more on negative happenings. reconfirmation, discussed in studies on the evil merry go around, refers to the fact that while we receive boosts of joyfulness from new positive happenings, over time, we get used to these happenings and they no longer have the same effect.

How can we counter this tendency to assign greater weight to the negative happenings in our life? A recent study by Sheila Cole and team-at a renowned university provides a clear explanation. Their study shows that discussing positive happenings leads to heightened well-being, increased overall life satisfaction and even more energy.

This studies may seem surprising because we are often reluctant to talk about our good fortune. We don't want to show off. Sometimes we don't want to attract bad luck to ourselves.. Or we possibly feel guilty that good things are happening to us in the face of the suffering in other people's lives; idle gossip and complaining, feeling negative or even wasting time and resources somehow feels like an appropriate, grounded escape, although erroneously . However,Ms. Cole and team's research suggests that describing our happy happenings to close friends and romantic companions is an important,helpful attitude for health and happiness. content with their lives. Share with those who care is a bold and joyousway of living which binds people together and can ultimately spread out as prescription for an entire community. Experts also found that, the more these people shared their joyfulness with someone on a given day, the happier and more satisfied they were on that day. To decide whether sharing joyfulness caused this boost in well-being, whether with a family member or a friend Those that share positive happenings and joyousness with other compatible people experience immediate, increased satisfaction and well-being, as compared to others who were not outwardly expressive and kept their news to themselves.

Well shared positive happenings give ourselves a boost and set up a trustworthy mindset where others can reciprocate their joyfulness as well.

Become aware of your dominant thoughts with the purpose of guiding them towards positive thinking. Your dominant thoughts embed themselves in your subliminal to create your beliefs and habits which translate into your actions and therefore create your reality. Review your thoughts, from time to time, to keep the happy and inspirational Regardless of the present circumstances, replace negative thoughts gently, lovingly with rousing, joyous, laughing, rejoicing thoughts-thoughts of love, peace, hope, compassion, winning and celebrations.

2.Write down, in order of importance, all your major strengths and your significant achievements till date. If you need prompting, ask a relative or a close friend to help with inputs for recalling traits and events and make this list complete with everything significant. Every day, preferably early morning or late in the evening,rewrite this list and read it to yourselfbecause repeating these in thought and spoken word will make a deep imprint of your positive aspects on your subliminal.

3.Think positively about yourself. Remind yourself that, regardless of your low, moderate or high status in life you are still a special, worthy and valued person, and that you deserve to feel good and content about yourself. Remind yourself that the Universe loves you and you love the Universe and that you are beautiful and peaceful in body, mind and spirit, just the way you are now. Your presence makes a valuable difference in the world, just because you exist.Instead of doing something greater than others,become a part of something greater than us. By attaching ourselves to an exemplery, beneficial cause, we are loved, loving and lovable. This book underlines deleting all negative thoughts about yourself from your consciousness, thoughts like : 'you are not good enough, not attractive enough or not wealthy enough. Replace negativity such as 'I make many mistakes" , or 'Not many people really like me with positive beliefs-and keep reinforcing:" I am important,lucky and fortunate, "I make a valuable difference in the world. To sum up:you are much more than just flesh and bones,You are a combination of mind,body,spirit,thoughts,emotions, confidence, self-worth high goals, so ,build yourself up-to a higher level than your human form(you being more than just flesh and bones; actuallyyou are a combination of mind, body,spirit,thoughts,emotions, higher ambitions) Importantly you are first a spiritual presence and the physical form second. Think in terms of being a magnificent expression of Divinity leading a human life.

4.Choose fresh, nutritious food as part of a healthy, balanced diet. Slow down while eating since meal times are special-even if you are eating on your work desk or alone. Switch off the computer/laptop/television, feel important by clearing the table and eat food slowly, with relish and gratitude.

5.Make it a regular habit to get enough sleep (aim for 7to8 hours). Instill joyous thoughts-thoughts of gratitude and thankfulness just before sleeping and right after waking up.

6.Clean and groom yourself regularly and well by taking showers, brushing your teeth and your hair, trimming your nails, keeping well-groomed and smelling fresh, wear clean clothes and use deodorants and fragrances as appropriate. Dressing up with style, finesse and finery will make you feel extra good about yourself. Within your wardrobe budgets and options , wear the nicest, cleanest, fashionable clothes-all this will keep your self-worth elevated.

7When you are done with work and social engagements, put on your walking shoes every day and go for a 10 to 15minutes walk either outdoors or in some indoor facility and work up a sweat doing cardio -workouts several times a week or as much as your doctor will allow.

8.Make it a habit of reducing your stress levels using basic, practical methods. It may be easiest to follow self-taught options , learn relaxation exercises like deep breathing outdoors,or some form of meditation which is easy to practice for you, yet effective. Do all these as often as you can. You may also find relaxation with hobbies as tending to and watering your plants or playing with and grooming your pets or other exciting hobbies that makes you relaxed and peaceful.

9.Bring out items that remind you of your achievements and your happiest, memorable times, of people special to you and display them where you and others can view them often-these are to nurture joyous memories and happy thoughts.(constantly replaying happy thoughts and memories sustains joy and improves the sense of self-worth.

10.Add on to your routine some more things that you enjoy. Find time to indulge in at least one or two pleasurable things every weekend.

11.Take up creative activities: any enjoyable form of singing, dancing, art, literary pursuits will bring out hidden, normally unexpressed talents and help you communicate with your intrinsic goodness and help communicate with others lovingly. Take part in your circle of friends, local community groups, with courses, programs accessible to you for all related activities.

12.Take interest in your friends' and community activities to lend a hand and help others using your talents, energy, enthusiasm, your caring nature. Make some time for these late evenings or on weekends, because taking interest in others and helping them out will be appreciated and people will be grateful to you. Send out joyful, helpful vibes and they will come back multiplied. It's important to remember that what goes around, comes around. Giving and receiving is an ongoing circle of positive, beneficial energies- you will receive attention, gratitude and respect from others.

Always be friendly, extra kind and gentle to yourself by appreciating yourself, being happy with all decisions that you have taken. In fact, congratulate yourself for taking the best life's decisions in the light of your aptitude, training and circumstances. Celebrate important achievements and milestones and be proud of your value and worth.

Keep company of people who are important in life and mean a lot for you. In addition, reach out to network to meet more like-minded people and expand your contacts and connections. Social media communities are a possible start to get introductions and accept more friends into your circle .Facebook, twitter , linked in are excellent resources; use them productively.

13.Stay away from negative people who draw you down and with whom you cannot build up healthy relationships. You have started focusing on family, friends and more like minded people, so you can let go ties with people you are not comfortable with.

joyfulness and vitality (level of energy and vibrancyfor life).

joyfulness, love and appreciation. who did notWhen sharing a positive experience, it is important to select a helpful listener.

To sum up: sharing our joy increases joy. Telling people about our joyfulness has far greater benefits than just remembering it or writing it down for ourselves. The process of discovering, enhancing and spreading joy starts to benefit ourselves first and when expanded further can benefit other as far out as 3 degrees of our social connections(ie benefiting our friends and that friend's friend and furthermore that friend's friend too and similarly keep compounding 3 degrees of connections for every close, appreciative and supportive friend , which will add unto thousands of people.In turn, others too can help support more people's joy by encouraging them to share their most positive happenings, and the things they feel grateful for. Supporting a friend or acquaintance's well-being in turn may enhance not only ourselves but other friends and acquaintances as well.

A study suggests that we have multiple times more positive happenings than negative. Why do we not emphasize on the positive events and build upon the past to experience similar ones in the future?What stops from experiencing, extending, and expanding our joy? Relevant research has been done and results may seem surprising because many people mostly hold back talking about their state of abundant lives. They feel others would get jealous because some get good things in life while a large majority get by with mediocrity and thousands-millions, around the world, even live poor lives. We do not want to attract bad luck. Sometimes we don't want to be our own bad omen We may even feel guilty that good things are happening to us in the face of mediocrity and suffering in parts of the world.

Dr Smith has shown that making daily lists of the things you feel grateful for—which helps draw our attention to the positive happenings in our lives—improves our psychological and physical health and well-being. For example, gratitude improves our ability to connect with others, boosts our compassionate nature, make us more optimistic and happy, reduces envy and greed and even improves health for people with physical ailments (even a major illness, for some people. It has been shown that by being grateful verbally we find others become loving and lovable, especially our family and friends and that we feel healthier and happier and it helps increase and sustain our well-being. Writing down and verbally expressing gratitude has faster and longer lasting benefits over just feeling grateful or, not feeling it at all. above and beyond simply feeling or writing down gratitude.

The experts found that people who habitually tend to talk to people they are close with about the good things that are happening to them also tend to feel happier and more satisfied with life. They also found that, the more these people shared their joyfulness with someone on a given day, the happier and more satisfied they were on that day. To decide whether sharing joyfulness caused this boost in well-being,a test group was experimented upon and in objective terms it turned out that t Those who shared positive experiences with their companions and friends experienced a greater uplifting well-being than those who did not share their experience with their companions.

To sum up: sharing our joy increases joy. Telling people about our joyfulness has far greater benefits than just remembering it or writing it down for ourselves. This well-being influences that of those around us, up to 3 In turn, we can help support others' joy by encouraging them to share their most positive happenings, and the things they feel grateful for. Supporting a friend or acquaintance's well-being in turn may impact not only ourselves but the well-being of all the people connected

we have three times more positive happenings than negative. What keeps us from fully capitalizing on all the good in our lives, making us experts have identified two main attitude that keep us from experiencing, extending, and expanding our joy: tendency to has shown that we tend to remember and focus more on refers to the fact that while we receive boosts of joyfulness from new positive happenings, over time, we get used to these happenings and they no longer have the same effect.

Their studies show that discussing positive happenings leads to heightened well-being, increased overall life satisfaction and even more energy.

This studies may seem surprising because we are often reluctant to talk about our good fortune. We don't want to overdo “ showing off” or we may feel guilty that good things are happening to us in the face of the others who are suffering in different parts of the world. Sharing happy happenings with significant others and close friends spreads cheer all around and makes us feel more satisfied. with life.

Many studies have shown that making daily lists of the things you feel grateful for—which helps draw our attention to the positive happenings in our lives—improves our psychological and physical health and well-being. For example, gratitude improves our ability to connect with others, increases our compassionate feelings and make us upbeat and more positive ; cutting down on envy and greed and even improves health for people with physical ailments (severe disease in one case). on gratitude to show that verbally expressing the gratitude we feel to people close to us helps increase and sustain our well-being above and beyond simply feeling or writing down gratitude. known that joyfulness

The experts found that people who habitually tend to talk to people they are close with about the good things that are happening to them also tend to feel happier and more satisfied with life. They also found that, the more these people shared their joyfulness with someone on a given day, the happier and more satisfied they were on that day. To decide whether sharing joyfulness caused this boost in well-being, the asked to write a positive experience or a neutral experience like a fact they had learned in class and either share it with their companion or not. Those that shared a positive experience with their companion experienced a greater boost in well-being than those who did not share topics of general nature) that enhance swell being.

. Sharing good news helps in a big way, though only people who are appreciative and at the very least good listeners. Staying away from nasty and negative people is a good idea in this context.

Another relevant tip is to share uplifting, joyous news as early as possible and convenient because over time it would loose its exciting and vibrant impact. networking happier and more satisfied with life. They also found that, the more these people shared their joyfulness with someone on a given day, the happier and more satisfied they were on that day. To determine whether sharing joyfulness caused this boost in well-being, experience or a neutral experienced a greater boost in well-being than those who did not share their experience with their companion or who shared a neutral experience with their companion. These findings suggest that it is the act of sharing joyfulness (and not of just thinking about joyfulness but not sharing it, or of sharing neutral information) that boosts well being.

One reason that the study asked The study group The study group to share their experience with close friends or romantic companions may come from the fact that these people may be more likely to support us. In the study's last experiment, the experts noticed that received constructive, encouraging, enthusiastic and positive messages after a successful experience (high achievement on a test) showed greater signs of joyfulness, love and appreciation. A worthwhile point to keep in mind is that as more and more joy is generated, we have to keep it away from it turning sour, mainly by being appreciative of this noble quality and secondly by not exposing or sharing it with negative people who may dampen the good effects of joyousness. A worthwhile point to keep in mind is that as more and more joy is generated, we have to keep it away from it turning sour, mainly by being appreciative of this noble quality and secondly by not exposing or sharing it with negative people who may dampen the good effects of joyousness. When sharing a positive experience, it is important to select a helpful listener.

them to share their most positive happenings, and the things they feel grateful for. Supporting a friend or acquaintance's well-being in turn may impact not only ourselves but the well-being of all the people connected

The experts found that people who habitually tend to talk to people they are close with about the good things that are happening to them also tend to feel happier and more satisfied with life. They also found that, the more these people shared their joyfulness with someone on a given day, the happier and more satisfied they were on that day. a positive experience with their companion experienced a greater boost in well-being than those who did not share their experience with their companion or who shared a neutral experience with their companion. These findings suggest that it is the act of sharing joyfulness (and not of just thinking about

When sharing a positive experience, it is important to select a helpful listener.

To sum up: by exchanging positive happenings, resulted in more joyfulness. Telling people about our joyous euphoria has far greater benefits than just remembering it or writing it down for ourselves. This study may also help clearly corroborate findings that have shown that our well-being influences others also,that of those around us, connected by three degrees of social networking . For going towards a long-term state of joyfulness, it's helping ourselves as well as others pursue not just for . In turn, we can help support others' joy by encouraging them to share their most positive happenings, and the things they feel grateful for. Supporting a friend or acquaintance's well-being in turn may impact not only ourselves but the well-being of all the people connected to winner. No wonder , joy has been defined as a divine virtue because it expands and benefits ourselves as well as the entire circle of like-minded people as and when we share joy.

The abundance of joy, from an unending, limitless source, is truly amazing!

This studies may seem surprising because we

are often reluctant to talk about our good fortune. We don't want to show off. Sometimes we don't want to attract bad luck to ourselves. Or we may feel guilty that good things are happening to us in the face of the suffering that exists in other people's lives. idle gossip and complaining, feeling negative or even gossip somehow feels more proper, practical and erroneously feasible. However, and colleague's studies suggests that describing our happy happenings to close friends and loved ones encourages and uplifts all concerned.

Many studies have shown that making daily lists of the things you feel grateful for—which helps draw our attention to the positive happenings in our lives—improves our psychological and physical health and well-being. For example, gratitude improves our ability to connect with others, boosts our compassionate nature make us optimistic and happier, decreases envy and materialism and even improves health for people with physical ailments (lung diseases disorders, in two patients). new study, however, extends studies on gratitude to show that verbally expressing the gratitude we feel to people close to us helps increase and sustain our well-being above and beyond simply feeling or writing down gratitude. Wisdom over the ages has recorded with conviction that joyousness expands through sharing.

Experts have found that people who often choose to relate with people they are close with about the good things that are happening to them also tend to feel happier and more satisfied with life. They also found that, the more these people shared their joyfulness with someone on a given day, the happier and more satisfied they were on that day Its been determined that sharing joyfulness caused re-resurgence well-being,health and vitality experience with their companion or who shared a neutral experience with their companion. These findings suggest that it is the act of sharing joyfulness (and not of just thinking about joyfulness but not sharing it, or of sharing neutral information) that boosts well-being.

Those who shared their grateful happenings with their companion reported greater satisfaction with life, joyfulness and vitality (level of energy and stamina).

When sharing a positive experience, it is important to select a helpful listener.

To sum up: sharing our joy increases joy. Telling people about our joyfulness has far greater benefits than just remembering it or writing it down for ourselves. This studies may also help partly explain studies by Rick Masters/ Ronald

Simmons Being enthused with joy within , by increasing its flow to radiate outwards and around to other people, we can positively enhance the lives of people who are inter-linked up to three degrees of connections away from us, thus reaching a wide circle of extended family, relatives and friends within several social circles and unto communities at large and located nearby or in other cities as well. All those affected can in turn, can help support each others, setting up a reciprocal supporting others' energies resulting in a multitude of people strengthening their healthy, happy living. awareness of healthy, happy living. Supporting a friend or acquaintance's well-being in turn may impact not only ourselves but the well-

Positive happenings occur every day, yet we don't always appreciate , recognize them and be grateful to the Universe. Most of us have so much to be thankful about and proud of, starting with an intact mind and body, food, water, sunlight, shelter and people close to us-with many more tangibles and intangibles, yet a rude remark from a stranger or our missing a preferred parking spot makes us highlight the negative over so many positive blessings. ? A study by Tom Harris and Pat Clooney suggest that we have multiple times more positive happenings than negative. What keeps us from openly realizing and appreciating on all the good in our lives, which is focusing on being happy instead of being stressed? experts have explained this oddity that keep us from experiencing, extending, and expanding our joy: the bitterness opinions and reconfirmation.; namely The bitterness opinions refers to our mind's innate tendency to give more weight to the negative; Adam Miller had found that we tend to remember and focus more on negative happenings. reconfirmation, discussed in studies on the evil merry go around, refers to the fact that while we receive boosts of joyfulness from new positive happenings, over time, we get used to these happenings and they no longer have the same effect.

How can we counter this tendency to assign greater weight to the negative happenings in our life? A recent study by Sheila Cole and team-at a renowned university provides a clear explanation. Their study shows that discussing positive happenings leads to heightened well-being, increased overall life satisfaction and even more energy.

This studies may seem surprising because we are often reluctant to talk about our good fortune. We don't want to show off. Sometimes by rejoicing about favorable events and good things that we have we don't want to attract bad luck to ourselves.. Or we possibly feel guilty that good things are happening to us in the face of the suffering in other people's lives; idle gossip and complaining, feeling negative or even wasting time and resources somehow feels like an appropriate, grounded escape, although erroneously . However,Ms. Cole and team's research suggests that describing our happy happenings to close friends and romantic companions is an important,helpful attitude for health and happiness.

CHAPTER SEVEN

Within us is a whole universe of possibilities. The Unified Field is the vastness of the common basic energy of the cosmos , an unending space of all traits, of unity, joy, positivist and neutrality. the unified field is the matrix or fabric of space time It is the essence of the entire spirit. There is no differentiation between consciousness and matter. As discovered by Pluto 2.500 years back and proven as the new version of reality recently consciousness and matter-they are both essentially intertwined and connected. which does not have dimensions of space and time but has the tendency to unify magnificent chemical and biological universe within each of us and connect us with the entire planetary universe. Infinite possibilities exist and freely circulate within the unified field. At the level of atoms and cells , we are constantly evolving and growing and the ideal state of being is to evolve and grow along in synchrization with infinite intelligence. everything. To connect with such infinite resources, we have to reach within, transcend to the core of our being instead of looking out for shooting stars at night to make wishes and hope that such wishes come true. The basic underlying force of the universe is a spiritual energy field of universal love, within which gravitational and electromagnetic fields, the strong and weak forces in the atom, and all other forces of nature, including time and space, are merely conditions of state. Within this spiritual realm of love, and near-death experiences are also conditions of state. The principal property of this field of love is its tendency to unite, complete and fulfill all living beings within a constantly evolving loving plan. This field of love is the absolute constant of the universe in that within it, time and space do not exist. Thus, we are instantly joined with the past, present and future of a universe which is in the process of uniting, completing and fulfilling itself.

The consciousness of the participant is the determining factor in being able to perceive the Unified Field, and the depth of one's sensory experience is what determines this consciousness. In that regard, our most profound sensory experience is the total surrender to what is deepest within ourselves, that is, the surrender to love and a joyful state of spirit consciousness - which is the awareness of an evolving loving plan and the taking of responsibility for one's function within that plan. The Unified Field is therefore a state of spirit consciousness. The blockage, which which may come in the way is ego consciousness.As individuals, we have to lift ourselves above the the ego consciousness level plane to the soul level or to the highest level to connect with the unified field(reach the enlightened state, which is the highest goal in human evolution)

..... loved for oneself and being seemingly separated from our original state of spirit consciousness and the Unified Field is of such deep spiritual proportions that, early in childhood, processes are triggered in the left brain which results in a partial brain imbalance and dominance as well as the denial, mistrust and forgetting of our connection to the Unified Field and the love and joy and a state of spirit consciousness deepest that the ego and ego consciousness is born - for survival and protection purposes only. death or

The base level of consciousness is the ego with the level of the soul above it and our highest level being the crown jewel. The ego can be compared to a protective outer shell that serves its purpose of protection for a predetermined period and is eventually meant to be shed. The individual consciousness is a sub-set of the unified field which can can be visualized as an unending lattice of electromagnetic energy coordinating all living beings within its energy field of co-existence, balance, harmony, love, joy, peace and goodness -encompassing lattice or fabric "The continuity of all goodness, joy and beauty lives within us all.

.

ABOUT THE AUTHOR

Positive Thinking Mentor&Author Gautam Sharma(gautamsharma.contact@gmail.com)- an intelligent, accomplished, capable,creative professional was born in India, has lived in Asia, Europe, Africa and now living in USA embodies and edifies positive thinking, power of optimism and is sharing insights into human behavior and human potential through philosophical, psychological perspectives with the view of sharing mankind's centuries-old wisdom plus proven, research findings so as to empower people worldwide. The author plans to utilize his strengths of professionalism,wide,varied experiences , creativity and communications' skills to publish the Empowerment Series on improvement, self help topics. Thank you valued readers for your continuous support , contributions and your favorable feedback. Wishing everybody abundance of positive thinking and better living through the power of optimism.

OTHER BOOKS BY THE AUTHOR

https://www.amazon.com/POSITIVE-THINKING-OPTIMISM-Original-English-ebook/dp/B01HRY684S/ref=asap_bc?ie=UTF8

also

https://www.amazon.com/SELF-CONFIDENCE-ESTEEM-HAPPINESS-SUCCESS-ebook/dp/B076VM1MNR/ref=tmm_kin_swatch_0?_encoding=UTF8&qid=&sr=

and

https://www.amazon.com/JOY-forHEALTHY-HAPPY-LIVING-Empowerment-ebook/dp/B078L6Y1YM/ref=sr_1_5?s=digital-text&ie=UTF8&qid=1515281796&sr=1-5

Discover your full potential: The Universe within

Gautam Sharma

(Dedicated to valued readers, especially those who write positive reviews)

Made in the USA
Coppell, TX
16 May 2021